The Bumps Ahead

The tale of a five-year pregnancy.

By Nick Finney

For Josh and Lily, because a book dedication is even more embarrassing than a hug from your dad in public.

Contents

Prologue

A man paces nervously up and down the waiting room of a maternity ward. Waiting for the midwife to come and tell him it is all over. Waiting to find out if he is the father of a girl or a boy. Waiting, so that he could rush off down to the pub, buy his mates cigars and wet the baby's head. It is a scene that used to be repeated all over the world back in the days before equality and common sense. Nowadays the father is very hands-on; well, as much as he can be, given he's not the one doing the hard work. As for me, I wasn't even near the hospital when my kids were born. But then again, I wasn't there when they were conceived either.

Chapter 1: Fifteen Million to One

On 4th July 1999, Posh and Becks were married by the Bishop of Cork at Luttrellstown Castle. The wedding was said to have cost over €1 million. Posh's tiara on its own, cost at least €30,000. Four weeks later it was our turn. For a fraction of the cost of that tiara, Lynn and I were married at the local church, with a reception at a nearby tennis club. The closest we came to having a celebrity at the wedding was when my brother drunkenly grabbed the microphone from the DJ and started singing George and Elton's 'Don't let the sun go down'.

We had just bought our first house together, a terraced three-bedroom place, on the borders of what was still considered to be a respectable area in North London. It was going to need a lot of doing up, but both sets of parents were already enlisted to help us. Aged 26, I had been in my job with a local glove manufacturer for three years. Lynn, who was five years older than me, was a sales office manager. We weren't going to challenge the Beckhams for wealth either, but we were doing OK.

We had already decided we wanted to start a family as soon as we were married. Moving from our one-bedroom flat into the house was the first stage. Lynn had come off the contraceptive pill a month or so before the wedding and we just assumed nature would take its course. In fact, during my groom's speech I'd commented that just as the Beckhams had named their eldest son Brooklyn after where he was conceived, we would be calling our firstborn 'multi-storey car park'. But, by the end of the year, nothing had happened. We didn't think anything was wrong; perhaps we just needed to time things better. Back then, there was no Google to consult, and from my perspective, I had spent my adult life trying not to get anybody pregnant, so I had little idea of how to increase the chances.

Lynn had started to investigate 'tips and tricks' through her friends mainly, and I was more than happy to go along with it at first. Being summoned home from work at lunchtime to 'have a go' whenever there was a full moon, or a high tide due; I was well up for that. Well, I was at first, but it soon became too mechanical and functional as we were only doing it because we had to. Sometimes I just wanted to eat my lunch in peace and not be a sex slave, but that biological clock was ticking.

The more this went on without results, the more technical it became. I had to make sure I was wearing loose-fitting boxers to avoid overheating, not drinking beer in and around the vital time frame, and not overexerting myself playing football or going to the gym. All of this added to the growing worry that something wasn't right, and it took the fun out of it. Each cycle would come and go, then we would have that unspoken period of hope, apprehension, and fear of the inevitable. When that moment came around, we would try to make light of it, but it started to nag.

'Is it me?'

'Why is it going wrong?'

At the same time, well-meaning friends and family couldn't help but ask the question, 'So when are you starting a family?' You can only deflect that question so many times before you just want to scream.

Back then, it was far less common for couples to have kids later in life. Literally, the minute you tied the knot, the clock was ticking. It didn't help that several close friends had also married around that time and were churning those babies out like there was no tomorrow.

Before we knew it, a whole year had passed. We were eight months into a new millennium. We took ourselves away for a holiday in Malta that summer, then on our return we decided it was time to make an appointment to see the doctor. Little did we know that we would be spending a lot of time with the medical profession over the next couple of years. Back then, I wasn't particularly nervous about seeking help, or worried about being asked embarrassing questions. I'd always been confident (well, more of a massive show-off really) and the thought of discussing my private parts with a female doctor seemed quite amusing.

October 2000. Our local doctor was the very first person to ask me for a semen sample. I was being told to have a play with myself. It still felt like a joke back then, but the underlying feeling was that the doctors know what they are doing; they will see what's up and will sort it out.

The first sample I ever did, I took into the surgery like a precious bird with an injured wing, nursing it carefully, wrapping the tube up in a sock to keep it warm. There was absolutely no way there was anything wrong with my sperm, surely? I was a proper bloke. I had worked in warehouses, lugging boxes about, sharing testosterone-filled jokes and challenges. I played football. I did all the things men do. I was all man, right?

A week or so later came the first real body blow of the journey. I had a low sperm count. A very low sperm count. The doctor was very matter of fact about it, but it really shocked me. She said I had pretty much no chance of getting anyone pregnant without significant assistance. What a kick in the balls, quite literally. With hindsight, I doubt there was a way to sugarcoat such news, but it was brutal to be told just like that.

I was still in a daze when I returned to work after that doctor's appointment. Someone asked if I was OK and I just broke down. I had to go and lock myself in a cubicle in the men's loo to try to regain my composure. Luckily for me, my best friend and best man at the wedding, Gregg, also worked with me. Someone had the wherewithal to let him know I was not in a good way, and he came to find me. Like an appallingly bad confessional, Gregg sat down in the cubicle next to me and listened to my snotty, snivelling description of what had gone on in the doctor's surgery. There was not much he could say or do, but he listened. Then he went out and made sure no one else would question me once I had regained my composure and made my way back to my desk.

That night at home we tried to make sense of it all. Why would I have a low sperm count? I was fit and healthy; I was always exercising; I didn't eat badly; I didn't smoke; I liked a drink but I wasn't exactly George Best; and there was no history in my family of this type of thing.

Over the next couple of days, as the shock wore off, I managed to find out some more information on the subject. A low sperm count is also called oligospermia, and a sperm count is considered lower than normal if you have fewer than 15 million sperm per millimetre of semen. That seemed like a lot to me. The way the doctor had broken the news though, it sounded like she had been able to count mine on one hand.

I certainly didn't have any of the physical symptoms that were described – pain in the groin, ejaculation problems or a lack of facial/body hair.

It was the environmental factors that scared me. Exposure to industrial chemicals or radiation was one of them. As part of my role at work, I had visited an irradiation plant which sterilised surgical gloves for us. I had been in the area where the radiation source was kept. Bloody hell, was that it? I knew it couldn't have been. The place was run to the absolute highest standards, and the source was under 40 feet of water, specifically to prevent contamination. But when you are searching for answers, then anything becomes possible, no matter how far-fetched it may seem.

What I should have focussed on was the fact that stress was an important factor too. We had been stressing ourselves out over this for months. Ultimately, I took solace in the fact that whilst having a low sperm count decreases the odds that one of your sperm will fertilise your partner's egg, it was still possible for men who have a low sperm count to father a child. There was still hope and lots of it.

Chapter 2: I Love You, Michael Owen

Though we had first seen the doctor in August 2000, progress felt slow. I suppose that given it was not cancer treatment or some other life-threatening situation, fertility investigation didn't get a lot of the NHS budget devoted to it.

Initially, we had to go over a lot of ground we had already covered independently. Tracking Lynn's fertility cycle obsessively, testing more sperm samples, trying a different diet, cutting out booze and trying not to let the stress of it all take over our lives. Everything else carried on as normal. We were still regularly asked about when we were going to have a baby, and apart from our close family, we had not told anybody about our predicament.

Through my work, I had enrolled on night classes that year, which was another thing to get stressed about. Every Monday and Wednesday from 6 pm to 9 pm, I was at the local college learning about marketing. There was also a lot of homework required. The house was a bit of a state given the lack of time I had to devote to DIY, but we made do with what we had. We had blown all the savings we had on desperately needed new double glazing.

We received some welcome, positive news in that the subsequent sperm count tests had begun to show an improvement in both number and mobility levels. Enough to warrant moving my status from complete waste of space to at least having a decent

11

chance of an assisted pregnancy. With this now an option, our doctor transferred us to the NHS for further infertility investigation, to give us some much-needed assistance.

Because I had been assessed as having a low count, there didn't seem to be as much focus on Lynn and whether everything was OK on her side. The main feedback we got in that regard, was that as she had been on the contraceptive pill for some years beforehand, there may be a delay, as that worked its way out of her system. She was ovulating and having regular periods, and hormone checks for progesterone appeared to be normal.

We had a couple of appointments at the local hospital in late 2000 and early 2001, but it seemed that we were going over old ground yet again. There was a bit more investigation this time around though, including blood tests and a scan for Lynn, just to check everything was where it was supposed to be.

Around this time, I had managed to tear my knee ligaments playing football, so had to have surgery. With the subsequent physio sessions, the college work, the day job and the fertility investigations, there was hardly time to draw breath most weeks.

By the time all the latest rounds of tests had been completed and reviewed, we were a quarter of the way into the year. Time was ticking by. However, by our next visit in April, our doctor suggested that, with my improved super sperm, we try IUI.

I didn't have a clue what IUI stood for, let alone how it worked. Intrauterine insemination (IUI) is one of the simplest forms of assisted fertility treatments. The aim is to increase the number of sperm that reach and fertilise the egg on their own. The technical jargon would say it involves placing sperm inside a woman's uterus to facilitate fertilisation. In layman's terms, you provide a sample (and trust me, by this time I was an expert at doing that), the specialists wash the sperm, pick out the best swimmers in the sample, and fire them up a tube into the womb. Like a wind-assisted sprinter, it's technically cheating, but you might just get a world record.

Having 'done the maths' with regards to ovulation and the peak window for fertilisation, we were asked to come in on Saturday 12th May 2001 at 4 pm.

I know exactly when it was because it was also FA Cup Final day. I am a massive football fan and avid Tottenham Hotspur supporter. The final of 2001 was being played between Liverpool and Tottenham's fiercest rivals, Arsenal. I was desperate for Arsenal to lose or I'd be suffering abuse from my Gooner-supporting friends for weeks afterwards.

The Cup Final was still a massive game back then too. It brought back memories of my childhood, when both BBC and ITV would have the game on, their shows starting at 9am; following the teams from their hotels to the stadium, singing 'Abide with me' and then recreating the key moments in the garden, or the local park, straight after the match was over. It was massive for me, and to be honest, the last thing I wanted to be doing was having to toss off into a jar when I could be watching football.

But needs must. I managed to watch the first half an hour before we had to make the relatively short trip to the North Middlesex hospital, a stone's throw from the Tottenham ground. Unbeknown to Lynn, I had snuck out a pocket radio. If I was not going to be able to watch the game, I'd at least be able to keep abreast of the score with that.

We arrived and met up with the team who would be performing the procedure. We had everything explained to us previously, but they ran through it all again in a calm, reassuring manner. I was listening, but my mind kept wandering to the Millennium Stadium in Cardiff. Please don't let those ***** win, please.

'Mr Finney... Mr Finney, are you ready?'

I was brought back into the room by the nurse. She was handing me one of those familiar sample pots.

'I'm afraid we don't have a room for you to use, so you will have to go to the gent's toilet and do the sample there.'

Bloody great. I joked that I was sure that George Michael got arrested for doing what I was about to do, but off I went with my pot and my secret radio.

Fortunately for me, the gents was empty when I entered, and I had the choice of the cubicles. This was the first time I had to produce a sample 'live'; previous ones had been done in the comfort of my own home. Now, here I was, in an NHS loo which had seen better days. Not very romantic or sexy, in any way, shape or form. If you have ever seen that scene in 'Train Spotting' where Ewan McGregor's Renton emerges from the toilet, well, where I was sent to perform was not much better. First things first, I switched the radio on low and listened for a minute or so, to try and get an idea of the score. For some reason, radio presenters never mention the score when you don't know what it is yourself. I was getting a bad feeling from the crowd noise and could sense the cockiness of 'that lot' coming across the airwaves at me. Finally, my fears were confirmed. Arsenal were 1-0 up with eight minutes left to play. Sod it.

This really did not help me focus on the job, that was quite literally in hand. I wouldn't be able to go out tonight, they'd be everywhere. Crowing, gloating, filling the pubs and signing in the streets. For Christ's sake, Liverpool, bloody do something. And they did. Suddenly little Michael Owen had burst the back of the Arsenal net with a volley from six yards out. YES!!!

Luckily, no one else was in the gents, as I let out a yelp of joy. I dread to think of how that would have looked to anybody else, particularly an officer of the law. I was sitting on the loo seat, trousers around my ankles, my little fella at half-mast, shouting at a tiny transistor radio. I'd knocked my sample pot over and had to scramble to retrieve it, before it rolled out under the door.

I realised I had been in the loo for quite a while and suspected that someone would be out to look for me soon. Sure enough, there was a knock on the outer door. Lynn. I flicked the radio off.

'Are you OK in there? You're taking your time.'

'Yep, I'm fine, it's just not the most relaxing environment to, you know...'

'Oh, do you want me to come in and help you? '

Blimey, I didn't want her coming in and finding my radio. She'd go mad!

'No, it's OK, I'll be done soon.'

Satisfied with my explanation, off she went. I didn't turn the radio back on. I had to get this sample done. I tried for a few minutes but whenever I thought I was getting there; the Cup Final came back into my head. This was ridiculous.

I checked my watch. There were about three minutes left. OK, I'll listen until full time, then there will be a break before extra time. I can be done and back in the consultation room before you know it. I flicked the radio back on low again.

'A long ball from Berger…. Owen races on to it, he's beaten Dixon for pace. Adams is covering, Owen turns him and shoots……. IT'S GONE IN! SURELY THAT'S IT!'

YES!!! I was ecstatic. As the clock ticked down, I got to work, sure that this was a sign from above that luck was on our side today. The final whistle blew and the sample pot filled in unison. We were going to have a baby boy, and he was going to be called Michel Owen Finney.

I had to suppress my joy when I went back to the consultation room. I'd totally forgotten that my part was the simple bit. Lynn now had to do her part which was a lot more uncomfortable. I wasn't invited to stay, so I went for a walk around the hospital grounds, listening to the after-match analysis and feeling happy, relieved, and lucky all at once. It just felt, right there and then, that everything was happening for a reason and this was going to work for us.

Chapter 3: Those Three Little Words

In. Vitro. Fertilisation.

Despite all those signs, Michael Owen was not our lucky charm. The weeks passed and nothing happened. Then Lynn had her period. IUI had failed.

We went back to the hospital and they told us that firstly, the NHS could only fund one round of IUI, and secondly, the quality of the sperm in the sample I had produced in May was not good enough to get positive results. We could pay to try again, but it was suggested that IVF was the next realistic step for us. We had been put on to the NHS waiting list, which would give us one free attempt at IVF, but the wait would be at least a year, more likely 18 months.

We had been saving up to get more stuff done around the house. Our kitchen was a state. We had a sink and a stand-alone gas cooker that was held to the wall with a chain. There were two gaping holes in the floorboards (from which field mice would frequently emerge and run riot around the ground floor) and where floorboards did still exist, I had nailed a patchwork of carpet remnants from my parents' house. The structure of the place was OK, but inside it looked like we were living in a squat.

We had a decision to make. Should we pay privately for IVF and continue living in squalor, or wait for the NHS to contact us in a year or so, and try to get on with our lives in the meantime?

Lynn was now 33 and felt that time was against her. We felt we had no option. We started to investigate private IVF clinics.

I guess things have come on in leaps and bounds, but back in 2001, it appeared that we did not have too many options. We were looking for places with decent success rates but affordable too. We met with a couple of service providers, but in the end, we were swayed by the London Women's Clinic. Not only were they based in prestigious Harley Street in London, but they had also been around since 1985 and had a good reputation and lots of success stories for us to take heart from. They were also offering a three-cycle package for £10,000. That was a new kitchen, a new bathroom, new carpets, pretty much a whole house makeover. But, at that point, having a baby trumped all those things. We had a few days away in Ireland booked for my 28th birthday in July, where we talked it over. Once we got back home, we made the payment to the clinic.

Our first cycle started in late August 2001. The clinic explained the process to us, and it seemed a bit lopsided and unfair on the woman. But then all it was doing was mirroring real life, where the man's element can be over in seconds.

There were half a dozen stages for Lynn to go through. First of all, they had to suppress her natural menstrual cycle, to make the medicines used in the various stages more effective. This was not pleasant as she had to give herself daily injections into her stomach. She did ask me to help but I was too squeamish. I had fainted at least twice whilst giving blood, I was not going to be poking needles into other people.

After two weeks of self-torture, came guess what? More injections.

This time it was to boost the number of eggs the ovaries produce, and it was done with a fertility hormone called follicle-stimulating hormone (FSH). The idea was that the more eggs the clinic could harvest, the more choice they'd have to pick the strongest.

Through this period, we had to visit the clinic every few days for Lynn to have blood tests (more needles) and scans to keep an eye on everything. Then a day or so before the egg collection? Another injection to help the eggs mature.

On D-Day, when they collected the eggs, yet more needles were involved. Lynn was sedated and the eggs were harvested using a needle, which were guided into each ovary by ultrasound.

While all these steps were taking place, as the male, I had the grand sum of nothing to do. It did make me feel like a spare part, especially as I could not even help with the injections.

However, D-Day also meant that my time had now come too, which meant filling another sample pot. After my experience in the toilets of the NHS hospital, it was not something I was looking forward too. However, given this was my sole task, and compared to what Lynn had gone through, I couldn't complain.

I was taken by a very nice nurse to a plush, softly lit room with a sofa and a bed in it. Complementing the furniture was a sizeable collection of adult magazines.

The nurse smiled at me. For a second, I thought she was going to stay in the room too, and I was about to make some smart-arsed quip about getting a first-class service, when she handed me my pot and told me to bring it back to her once I was done. The door closed and I was left alone in a teenager's paradise. All that was missing was a games console.

I probably spent far too much time checking out the titles on show, deciding which one to go for. Then two things struck me; firstly, that I was not there for fun, I had a job to perform and secondly, how many other dirty sods had been touching these magazines, and had they washed their hands?

The novelty of the surroundings quickly wore off and I duly produced my sample. I made my way back to the nurses' station, overly exaggerating the act of drying my freshly washed hands, and handed my precious cargo back in. For the money we were paying, those boys had better bloody work, I thought.

That was it, my part in the process was over. The sample was taken, washed and spun at a high speed to isolate the healthiest and most active sperm for selection. This certainly put a new spin on a Siemens washing machine in my mind.

With this done, we were free to go home while the clinic went to work on fertilising the eggs. For our first cycle, this was done simply by mixing the selected sperm with the eggs and letting nature take its course. Lynn was sent home with some pessaries, to help prepare the lining of the womb to receive the embryo. She did have the choice of some more self-administered injections, but with her stomach now resembling a pub dartboard, she declined.

Three days later, we were back in Harley Street for the embryo transfer, which, compared to some of the other parts of the process was straightforward. A catheter was used to transfer it straight into the womb.

It was at this stage that we learnt something that had likely been affecting us all along; Lynn's eggs were mainly granular in shape. I didn't know this at the time (why would I?) but all women are born with their eggs already in them. 'Good' eggs are smooth and ovular in shape, which allows them to adhere to the lining of the womb. A granular egg has less chance of success, especially when paired with a low sperm count. It all made sense now and I think in a way it helped us in knowing that we were equal. Neither of us was the one who could not conceive, it was unlucky that we were both slightly under par.

Unfortunately, the clinic also reported that my sperm sample quality had dropped again, and they had trouble getting many high-quality prospects from it. We were warned not to get our hopes up and encouraged to focus on the fact that we had two more chances. The clinic had learnt a great deal from cycle one that could be used to improve our chances for cycles two and three.

We left the clinic with the embryo in place, and despite what we had been told, quietly confident that this would be the one. After all, it was in place and in effect; Lynn was now pregnant. All was going to be good with the world. This was on 10th September 2001. Just a day later, whilst our hope was still there, everything changed on planet Earth.

For the next two weeks, we waited, our minds flicking from pregnancy to the terrible atrocity that had taken place in New York and shocked the world. The clinic had advised Lynn to take a pregnancy test two weeks after the transfer. Sadly, it was not necessary as she had her period shortly before, confirming that the cycle had been unsuccessful. With everything else happening in the world, our tragedy did not really seem that bad in comparison. But it was still our tragedy and we did feel it.

Our next attempt was set for mid-November. The clinic suggested that as the issue with the eggs was now known, they would implant two embryos this time. This would double the chance of success, but the flip side was the possibility of twins, triplets or more.

Just after our first cycle ended, my boss resigned. He had told the company he was changing career to become a football coach but had instead set up a rival company. This caused a lot of unrest and grief, and I was implicated in the deceit as I had worked on projects with him, which unbeknown to me, he had been setting up for his new venture.

As the preparation work came about again, I was torn between travelling into London with Lynn and dealing with the fallout at the office. I felt very let down by what had happened. The owners of the business fully backed me, but I wanted to get my version of the truth out to some of the key customers who had also been embroiled in what had gone on. Lynn, ever the trooper, insisted that I didn't need to travel with her every time. So, while she made several trips alone, I was off in Liverpool, Leicester and Derby trying to right some wrongs. This also felt wrong, but for my own sanity, I needed to have my say. The whole thing ended up heading towards court where I was going to be a key witness. Yet more stress, and something I could have done without. Fortunately, a last-minute compromise was reached, and I got my vindication.

Whether this had any effect on the failure of the second cycle, we will never know. By the time the embryo extraction/fertilisation was due, it was early December. Lynn had been alone for the majority of the pre-visits and I was stressed to the hilt. Again, the clinic reported that my sperm count was lower than a snake's belly. Subconsciously I think we both had little hope this time around. With our appointment being early in the morning, we chose to go into London to do some Christmas shopping after we had finished at the clinic.

Inevitably Lynn's period came again. We were saddened, but not as much as we were the first time around. Knowing that we still had one more attempt left to take place in January 2002, we tried to enjoy Christmas with our families and not think too much about anything else.

Having managed to save a bit of money since handing over our savings to the clinic, we also used the holiday period to start doing some much-needed work on the house.

By early January 2002, we were back on the IVF treadmill for the third and final time with the private clinic. There had been no word at all from the NHS so if this didn't work, we were not sure how long it would be until we got another bite of the cherry.

On 16th January 2002, two more embryos were fertilised and implanted. I felt a bit like Charlie Bucket; we had already bought two chocolate bars with what money we had, but neither had contained the Golden Ticket. We were down to our last chance now. Was this the bar we would slowly unwrap and catch a glimpse of gold?

Two weeks later we were back at the clinic. Lynn hadn't started her period, which was further than we'd got before, so the doctor wanted to give her a blood test to measure levels of hCG (a hormone called human chorionic gonadotropin). Having hCG in the bloodstream usually means a positive pregnancy test. The test proved inconclusive, as the hormone can still be present after a miscarriage, but we sensed that this was just the news being broken to us gently. We arranged to go back in a week. In the end, we didn't need to bother. Lynn's period started and we were done. It was an awful feeling. We couldn't do any more. We could not afford to do any more. If we had been told the odds before we started, perhaps we might not have thrown £10,000 at it. But we had done. That was the price of a family and we had paid it, only to see the chance slip away like sand through our fingers.

The next few months were a bit of a blur. Life returned to some sort of normality. I had recovered enough to begin playing football again on Saturdays, which was a great stress buster. Being out on that pitch was enough to make me forget anything and everything for 90 minutes. I wasn't very good at it but that wasn't going to stop me trying. We went out with friends, made progress on the house, even got asked to babysit our niece and nephew a few times. It was good that people weren't treating us with kid gloves.

By August, we had saved enough money (supplemented by an interest-free loan from the bank of mum and dad) to get a new kitchen fitted and take a holiday with two close friends, Alison and Terry. They were in the process of moving to a new house at the time, but their chain had been disrupted, leaving them without a home for a few months. We got on so well that we offered to put them up in the interim. They were a little apprehensive at first; Alison was three months pregnant, and with what we had just endured they did not want to rub it in. We were adamant it was fine; it wasn't going to be the elephant in the room.

It turned out to be a very positive time for us. We all got on well and having Alison with us every day helped normalise pregnancy, reducing the stigma we may have subconsciously held about our situation. We were actually a little sad when they completed their house move in early November. They were only moving a couple of miles away, but we would miss their company. Our disappointment was short-lived though, as a few days after we had helped them transfer their belongings into their new abode, we received the call up from the NHS.

Chapter 4: Those NHS Heroes

At the end of November 2002, after 11 months on hold, we received a letter from the NHS. It invited us to a consultation at the Homerton hospital on 16th December.

After all that time trying not to think about it, the nerves and emotions quickly came flooding back. From a personal perspective, I was finding it hard to comprehend how, if a professional private clinic couldn't help us get pregnant, the NHS somehow would. In my mind, private meant higher quality. I had so little concept of just how good our National Health Service was at this point. I'd been lucky enough not to have had many dealings with it, so most of what I went on was what I heard in the press. Overworked, underfunded, undersupported; I couldn't reconcile how they would be able to compete with the Harley Street clinic.

My impressions quickly began to change during that first meeting in December. The Homerton had obtained our records from the private clinic and thoroughly reviewed them in advance of our meeting. We were asked in detail about what happened in each of the three attempts at IVF, so that the doctor could put some of the data into context.

It was agreed that there would be two major changes to the way things had been approached privately. Firstly, we would have three eggs implanted. For the last private IVF attempt, we had two implanted, despite increasing the chances of having twins, triplets or more, which would pose serious risks to the health of both Lynn and the babies. This was the last roll of the dice and we were not going to pay for any more private IVF. Added to this, the knowledge that the eggs were going to have trouble attaching to the womb, greatly reduced the chance of multiple pregnancies.

Secondly, the doctor said that they would carry out intracytoplasmic sperm injection (ICSI). To me, this sounded like a spaceship, a sports car or an adult movie title, but it is a technical procedure, where if there are issues with the sperm quality, such as low motility or numbers, a single sperm is injected into the egg by an embryologist. This was not something we'd been offered privately. We could only assume that it was a significant additional cost and not part of the package we had signed up for.

So, the NHS was not that non-league compared to the private premier league after all. Heartened by our discussions, and with a start date of mid/late January agreed, we went home and enjoyed our Christmas break. 2003 felt like it was going to be a good year.

Chapter 5: 2003: The Big One

By now we were old hands at this IVF lark. All that had changed was the journey to the hospital, and the fact that my Y-registration Daewoo Leganza didn't look as out of place in Homerton as it did in Harley Street.

I still can't explain why, but we just felt more relaxed working with the NHS as opposed to the private clinic. It seemed more genuine (and it was free). Alison had also just given birth to a beautiful girl who'd been named Evie, and I was honoured when asked to be her godfather. Everything felt good.

After a couple of weeks of those pesky injections, Wednesday 5th February came around and it was egg collection time. Our appointment was bright and early, at 8 am. Of course, being the NHS, I was back in the toilets to provide my sample, but with no football to distract me I gave a professional, workmanlike performance and proudly returned my pot to the nurse, maybe a little too quickly to impress her.

The doctor reported that the ICSI process had worked well and three embryos had been successfully implanted.

We went home and waited. We tried not to get stressed about it but given the precarious nature of things every time Lynn moved, I was anxious. At one point she tripped over the back doorstep and landed on her backside. Straight away we both felt sick to the stomach, and the next 24 hours were painful (and not just for her bruised behind); but nothing terrible happened and we relaxed a little.

Our next appointment was set for Friday 21st February. We were due in at 8 am. We were wide awake long before sunrise and we just couldn't wait to get into the hospital and have the test. There had been no bleeding, no sign that things had gone wrong. We still had a home pregnancy test kit. Lynn tried it and we sat in the bathroom staring at it. Slowly but surely, a faint blue line began to emerge in the window. There was some screaming, some reading of the user information sheet and some crying. We were pregnant.

Chapter 6: A Brief Moment of Happiness

We were at the hospital a good half an hour before our appointment, eager to receive confirmation of what we thought we knew. It felt like a dream. Blood samples were taken and tested; and the raised hCG levels reaffirmed it. The team were genuinely pleased for us. I can't remember exactly what they were telling us, because I spent most of the appointment blubbing. The one thing I did recall was the doctor explaining to us that we'd need to return for further blood tests to ascertain, through the hCG levels, if more than one of the embryos had taken. At that point we really didn't care if it was one, two, three, hell ten babies; we had finally done it after almost four years of trying.

Once we got back from the hospital, we had to do the rounds and let our family know. I typed up a note for my mum and dad which simply said 'Congratulations, you're going to be grandparents'. This was mainly as I knew I wasn't going to be able to start the sentence, let alone finish it, without bursting into tears. In fact, I burst into tears before I even handed the letter over. There were tears, hugs, and tea all round. We then went over to Lynn's parents, once her dad had finished work, and this time Lynn led the crying. Then it was on to Lynn's sister's, though by this time I was all cried out and it was beer time with my brother-in-law, rather than more gallons of tea.

It was probably one of the most emotionally charged, joyful days we experienced. One where everything felt pure, where we had no thought or fear that things could go wrong. We'd got what we had been fighting so desperately for, and we wanted to celebrate it.

We attended Lynn's annual work's dinner in Birmingham the following night. Only a couple of her closest friends knew of our good news, so Lynn had to play ill when she was asked why she was not drinking. As it was a free bar and I was celebrating, I made sure I drank for two.

On Monday 24th February we were both back to work. We'd decided not to tell anyone else outside the immediate family and closest friends until we got further down the line. Most 'normal' pregnancies are not announced until at least 12 weeks, so we would have to keep it to ourselves for another 8-9 weeks.

We were barely a few hours into our vow of silence when things started to go wrong. Lynn called me in a panic. She'd started bleeding. That familiar 'pit of the stomach' sick feeling came back immediately. We called the Homerton and they told Lynn to come in as soon as possible. To save time, Lynn's oldest friend Lisa, with whom she also worked, drove her straight from the office to the hospital. They took some blood and checked the hCG levels. More importantly, they calmed us down. It wasn't entirely unusual, and the hormone levels were still on the way up from the previous Friday. Lynn was sent home and told to rest and try to relax. The next morning, we both went back to the hospital. The bleeding had stopped and again the hCG levels were higher than the previous day. Maybe we had been worrying over nothing.

The following day, Wednesday 26th February, the bleeding started again. We tried not to panic this time and were reluctant to call the hospital again for fear of sounding like pests and losing their goodwill and help. In fact, they couldn't have been more helpful and caring. As there was nothing serious happening, they told us to sit tight, try and keep calm and stay in touch with them. No question or worry would be too stupid.

So that's what we did. We sat at home and waited. It was awful to feel so helpless, but there was absolutely nothing either of us could do. Time slowed down. Every time Lynn visited the toilet, it was heart-stopping.

After a sleepless night, we had to endure it all over again. As the day wore on, the bleeding started to increase again. I cannot explain how desperate the feeling was; slowly seeing your dreams slipping away. We called the hospital and they asked us to come the next morning.

Again, we were there bright and early, though unlike last time when we were inspired by excitement, this time we were driven by fear and pain.

Lynn's blood was taken again, and we faced a wait while they checked it. The bleeding had slowed once more. We were fearing the worst. We didn't think there was a best to hope for. But there was.

Lynn's hCG had risen again despite the bleeding. The doctor left this statement hanging for a few seconds while it dawned on us. More than one of the embryos had taken. We may have lost one over the last few days, but we were still pregnant.

We left the hospital with a mixture of different feelings. We had lost our baby. OK, biologically it was still just a bundle of cells, but from that moment on the previous Friday in our bathroom, he or she was our baby. But he or she had a brother or sister, and that little fighter was still hanging in there. We had to be thankful for that.

We were going to try and relax over the weekend and take stock of things. Saturday passed uneventfully until around 6 pm. Then the bleeding started again.

At first, it was slow; just spotting really, but by Sunday morning it was enough for us to realise we were losing our other baby. We called the hospital and were asked to go in on Monday. We went for a walk to try and clear our heads. We knew where this was going, we just wanted it over now. Nature was being too spiteful to us.

Monday morning came and we were back at the Homerton for blood tests and a scan. Rather than put us through the torture of hanging around the hospital, it was arranged for our own doctor to give us the results later in the day. At 4 pm on 3rd March, our worst fears were confirmed. The hCG levels had dropped and a miscarriage had occurred.

We both stayed off work the next day. We went for a walk around Hampstead Heath. It was something we always liked to do to cheer ourselves up. Sometimes you might see a celebrity wandering about. That day, however, if I'd bumped right into George Michael, I would not have noticed. The last ten days had been an emotional rollercoaster in the extreme. It didn't seem real. How could life be so cruel, to give you such joy then only to snatch it away, not once, but twice in the space of a matter of hours?

On Wednesday 5th March we went back to the Homerton to confirm what we already knew. As always, the team there were brilliant with us, two emotionally wrecked human beings. We agreed to a follow-up appointment in a few months' time once the raw emotion of the last few weeks had settled a little bit.

Chapter 7: What Next?

In one sense, it was a relief that it was all over. There was no more false hope to be had. For almost four years we had lived our lives with that flame of hope in sight. Gradually it had dimmed and waned, but while we could still see it, there was still a possibility. We had made a lot of sacrifices and put our lives on hold during that time. Yes, we had made progress on turning the house from a squat to a home, but we were still using our garden furniture as our dining table and chairs, and there was still a lot to do. When I think back to that period it always reminds me of a line from The Streets' song 'Dry your eyes':

'And I'm just standing there.

I can't say a word.

Cause everything has just gone.

I've got nothing.

Absolutely nothing.'

We did have a lot to be grateful for, but it didn't feel like it. I thought back to a time several years before, when I'd found out that my then-girlfriend had been seeing a mutual friend behind my back. I was furious and ended up being chucked out of a local pub after confronting them EastEnders' style. An older friend, Russ, had taken me back to his house to sober me up and calm me down. While I sat there simmering, he said something that has stuck with me.

'This might feel like the end of the world right now, but it's not. Everything happens for a reason, and one day you'll realise what that reason is.'

At our wedding reception, Russ and I shared a moment where no words were needed. He had remembered that night as well as I had. He just gave me a smile that said, 'See, I told you so.'

I tried to seek solace in that. Russ had been spot on then, but right now I couldn't see what the reason could be for life treating us so cruelly.

I threw myself into everything else in my life to try and 'fix' what I could fix. I pushed ahead with work on the house, painting, decorating, plastering, building furniture; I was on it. With my football club, I played every game I possibly could, for any team that would have me (mainly the lower ones). I even earned myself a championship winners' medal with our 6th team, scoring in the game that won us the league. I partied. A lot. A couple of times I woke up under my car or in a bush, covered in kebab and scratches.

At work, I had the perfect project to keep me occupied. We had purchased another glove company based in the Midlands. My bosses had enough faith in me to give me a key role in integrating this business into ours. It was full-on but very interesting. I was up and down the M1 every week, staying over quite often as I learnt about our new products and processes. I also discovered a lot about life during those months.

I had gone into the acquisition feeling important and probably a little bit cocky. Having met and befriended many of my new colleagues, I was then overwhelmed with sadness and guilt when we started to make them redundant, as we streamlined their business and brought it into line with our own. Having that sort of power over others is not a toy, and it taught me a lot about humility. These people were not in control of what was happening to them, but they dealt with it in a dignified manner. I, on the other hand, was too self-absorbed.

Subconsciously, I had reacted to what was happening with the IVF, by building a shell of overconfidence around myself. When it had finally failed, I had thrown myself into everything with the same attitude. That was fine when I was playing football, as I wasn't harming anyone. With the drinking, I was only harming myself and the bushes I fell into. But with work, I had a responsibility to do the right thing.

Lynn was also going off the rails. She was out drinking with friends after work too often, and unbeknown to me at the time, she had run up a hefty bill on a credit card she had in her name. We were not talking to one another much and were living separate lives. Eventually, I asked her friend Lisa to help me try and talk sense to her. It all ended in a massive row, but that row helped clear the air. All the hurt, frustration and anger of the last few months came out. Though we'd talked about what had happened, we hadn't listened to one another, as we were each caught up in our own sadness.

The real turning point came in June 2003 when we went on a family holiday to Portugal. We had hired a villa for two weeks between Lynn and me, Lynn's parents, and Lynn's sister's family – Jill, Malcolm and their two kids Alex (almost four) and Chloe (just turned two).

It was a wonderful two weeks of laughter, sun, food and talking. Lynn and I got to spend a lot of time with Alex and Chloe, and it was very cathartic. I realised that I'd just blocked out the thought of being a dad. I think Jill and Malcolm must have loved being able to take some time off, but we loved being able to look after the kids; play with them and mess around at dinner time to get them to finish their food. Basically, play at being parents.

Shortly after coming back from that brilliant holiday, we were back at the Homerton for our follow-up to the events in March. We were not sure what to expect or what might be on offer. Perhaps there might be another chance to try for IVF?

At 3.45 pm we met with our doctor for what would be the final time. He explained to us that we couldn't have another try at IVF on the NHS. He could take us on privately, but he genuinely didn't want to take our money for what would be a hopeless mission. He was very frank, but it was what we needed right then.

He suggested that we should go on holiday (my tan was clearly not that impressive) and then think about looking into adoption.

Chapter 8: Life Begins

For the next few weeks, we started to devote some time to investigate adoption. It hadn't been something we had considered before, as we had been so focussed on starting a biological family. It was also something neither of us were very clued up on. In my mind, adoption conjured up images of evacuees, or orphans, being sent from London to some obscure part of Wales, to live on a farm. Babies being left in a church doorway, with the vicar hearing their cries and coming to their rescue. It was a very far cry from that. In 2003, 4,821 children were adopted in the UK (according to the office of national statistics) and many thousands more were not living with their birth families, for a variety of reasons.

Adoption was officially introduced into the UK in 1926, although it would have taken place before then, but there was no formal system or rules to be guided by. Back then, it sounded like a swap shop where unmarried mothers had their children taken from them to provide 'relief' (although I suspect it was more to save the shame of an unmarried mother in the family). The children would then be placed with couples who were unable to conceive. The interests and welfare of the children themselves seemed to be an afterthought, at best.

It was as late as the year 2000 when the government carried out a review of the adoption process and launched 'a new approach' - well, it was 'new' Labour after all. This approach radically changed how adoption was handled, with the focus on increasing transparency. I had heard tales of people not finding out that they had been adopted until they were adults, and in some cases, only finding out by accident. By 2003, it was all about making the child aware from as early an age as possible, so that it wasn't a dirty secret.

Therefore, we were entering a world where the experts were also learning new ways of working.

Initially, we were reticent about approaching our local council's adoption team. With a population of just over 300,000 people, there was a very good chance we could bump into our child's birth family every week, which would have been very stressful.

It was then that we had our first moment of enlightenment. I discovered that a guy, who often had a few beers with lads I knew, had recently adopted a boy and girl, with his wife. Incidentally, once you start looking into adoption, it is amazing how many people have adopted, have been adopted or know someone who is adopted.

Anyway, in late September 2003, we were all invited to a mutual friend's birthday drinks evening. I had asked this guy if it was OK for Lynn and me to have a chat with him and his wife. After the initial introductions, we wore the pair of them out, spending the next hour or two peppering them with questions. To be fair, they were fantastic and opened our eyes to many areas we had yet to explore. We truly were naive about this adoption lark, but then I guess any first-timers would be, given it is not your first option when it comes to starting a family.

We learned that you didn't have to adopt via your local council. You could seek advice from them, but you could go to any area in the UK if you wanted to.

We were advised to look at the inner London boroughs. It was a simple but sad fact; the more deprivation and hardship there was in an area, the more children there were likely to be in a position where adoption was their only real hope of a better life.

In some ways that may sound like a callous approach, but it's a fact of life. We learned for the first time of the cycle of events which occurs in these areas. A young girl falls pregnant at an early age. She is supported by social workers and they do all they can to keep mother and child together, but more often than not, this fails. The child is taken into care and the girl, devastated to lose her child, but also missing the attention and feeling of being important, falls pregnant again within a short space of time. So the cycle repeats itself.

That evening we talked about adoption in almost business-like terms; the law of supply and demand meant that adoptive parents were sought after in these boroughs, waiting times were much shorter, and there was a much greater chance of getting a younger child, which is really what we wanted. Though I did have visions of some heavily-bearded 16-year-old turning up and drinking all my beer.

44

Armed with this information, we were able to identify exactly which borough we wanted to approach to maximise our chances of a swift and successful adoption attempt. Greenwich.

Chapter 9: South of the Border

In general, North Londoners don't like going to South London. South Londoners don't much care for North London. I'm not sure if that's a tribal football thing or the fact that it's such a bloody ball-ache to do. You can go through central London and cover 20 miles in two and a half hours, or you can take a 70-mile detour around the M25 and arrive in two and a half hours. Take your pick.

That was the first thing I noted on our initial drive to the borough. We were going to be spending a lot of time in the car if we chose to move forward with our adoption plans here. I had written to the Greenwich adoption team on 17th October 2003. It was a simple letter, but one that would change our lives in the coming months.

'Dear Sir/Madam,
My wife and I are very keen on adopting and we would like to put ourselves forward to Greenwich as prospective candidates to adopt.

We would be very grateful if you could advise us on what the next step is from here.

We can be contacted at the address/phone number above, or by mobile (07976 *** ***) or email: nick.finney@***.co.uk

We very much look forward to hearing from you soon.

Yours sincerely,'

We had received a letter back a couple of weeks later inviting us for an initial chat on 9th December. I couldn't ever recall having been to Greenwich before, nor could Lynn, so we decided to take a trip the weekend before to check things out.

Fortunately, the drive wasn't quite as bad as I had feared. Whilst playing football in South London, I'd endured some absolute nightmare travelling experiences, but that was more down to well-meaning teammates taking charge of the A to Z and leading us through the very centre of the city. Our journey that afternoon skirted around the Capital itself, but we still got the buzz of seeing all the major landmarks that Canary Wharf had to offer.

We found some parking and walked into the main shopping centre which was bustling with pre-Christmas shoppers. It was freezing cold and despite the festive buzz, I immediately felt like an outsider. I also noticed that I was studying every person who was pushing a buggy or pram around. It was strange to think that we could be walking past our future son or daughter and be totally unaware. It also felt a little unnerving that we were on the birth family's territory, even though we didn't yet know them, and they would never really know us.

Once I realised that I wasn't going to be hung, drawn and quartered for being 'from the North', we went about getting our bearings. We found the adoption team offices and located the best parking place for when we next came down. We went for a bit of a shop ourselves. Amazingly they had all the same shops as we did and everything!

The main thing that struck me on that visit was that Greenwich is no different from our town. From the discussions we had back in October, I had built this stereotyped image of the inner London boroughs being full of young girls who looked like Vicky Pollard from Little Britain, pushing multiple buggies around, whilst chain-smoking and swigging from a two-litre bottle of White Lightening Cider. The adoption journey was going to be a steep learning curve for a middle-class boy, who had never experienced hardship or been denied the privileges that his upbringing automatically gave him.

On Tuesday 9th December, we returned to Greenwich for our initial 'get to know you' meeting with the adoption team manager, Florence. It lasted a couple of hours and was as much about us feeling comfortable with the journey ahead, as it was with the adoption team checking our suitability; that would come later anyway.

Florence told us that there were five stages to the process. Stage one we had already completed, in the sense that we had decided that we wanted to adopt, and we had sought out information to bring us to this meeting.

We were asked about how we had got to this point, including the overall time involved. Although this was just an initial meeting, there was an understanding that even just considering adoption could not be a knee-jerk reaction to other means of starting a family failing. The fact that our last IVF attempt had failed ten months previously was definitely in our favour.

Stage two was registration and initial checks. We had to sign up with the adoption agency which we felt was right for us. As far as we were concerned, Greenwich was the one for us and we had no intention of looking elsewhere. Greenwich would then run some background checks (criminal records and so on) and get some references as part of the initial evaluation process. If we couldn't pass that, there was no point in carrying on.

Stage three was where the going got tough - training and assessment. Our social worker would help to assess our situation and suitability, so that they could report to the Adoption Panel for acceptance of us as prospective parents. This process could take several months and would involve numerous home visits to assess all manner of things. Our mental state, our physical suitability, what support network we could rely on, and if our house was safe for a child to live in. There would also be training sessions with social workers where we would be alongside other prospective adopters. It all sounded daunting.

If we survived stage three, the next level was where the good stuff started to happen, matching us with the right child. There was another panel for this part of the process which would take into consideration family history on all sides, ethnicity and generally making sure you were a good match to ensure a successful 'partnership'.

After that came the final piece of the jigsaw; meeting your new child and having them move in with you. There would be a series of visits planned, initially you would visit them in their environment, then when they had got used to you, you would have them for short stays to make the transition as comfortable as possible.

Once all that was done, with integration successfully completed and all was well in the world, then you could apply to become the child's legal parents.

Florence was very straight-talking and warned us that this was not going to be an easy ride. With hindsight, her words were designed to sort the wheat from the chaff. Those who were not fully focussed, and determined that this was what they wanted, would think twice about embarking on something so stressful, invasive and emotional. Florence told us not to decide there and then, but to go home and talk it over. She would do likewise with her team, and we would reconvene in a few days on the phone to see if we were truly up for the fight.

That evening, over a Chinese takeaway, we discussed the events of the day. Yes, Florence had made it very clear that it was going to be a difficult journey, but we'd already been through too much pain and heartache to just give up now. We were in it for the long haul, no matter what.

Chapter 10: 2004: An Adoption Odyssey

Having confirmed to Greenwich that we were ready to start the adoption process, and had filled in an initial application form, we were advised that wheels were now in motion with a likely start date of February 2004. This gave us six to eight weeks to enjoy life as we knew it.

We booked ourselves a week away in Morocco immediately after New Year, for a bit of winter sun. I was naively taken in by the daytime temperatures shown in the holiday brochure and ended up having to wear pretty much everything I'd packed most nights as the pleasant 22°C heat turned to 3-4°C after sunset. But we had a good week. We enjoyed sitting and reading, commenting that the next time we came away would be very different.

The holiday continued when we got back to the UK. Lynn's mum and dad had recently moved from just around the corner from us, to live by the sea in Margate. It was something they had always wanted to do, so once they had both retired, they sold their flat and bought a lovely two-bedroom bungalow in a little village called Garlinge. They had also celebrated retirement by taking a six-week extended Christmas break in Tenerife. So, for the first few weeks of the year, we were spending our weekends housesitting and getting to know the area. It was strange being at the seaside when the beach was covered in snow, but we immediately felt an affinity to the town. I even started to follow Margate Football Club, which was just a stone's throw away from the bungalow.

During those weekends, we would go out for a drink or food in the evening and talk about what was about to happen. Was our child born already? Would we be able to have a baby rather than an older child? What would they look like? How would it feel to meet them for the first time? It was scary but exciting all at once.

At the end of January, we received a letter from someone who would go on to play a big part in our lives, Sue. Our first meeting was set for the 16th February. We may as well have been having the Queen come to visit, such was the level of nervousness. We spent the weekend beforehand cleaning the house within an inch of its life, desperate to show Sue that we would be ideal parents because a child could eat their dinner off our floor. Cushions were plumped over and over, pictures of our niece and nephew were put in positions of prominence to show just how much we loved them. Sue had probably seen this a thousand times before, but organising the house kept us focussed and in control.

Sue was brilliant from the offset. We were looking at the process as if we were being put through an examination, one wrong move and we would be out on our ear. Sue was looking at it in an entirely different way; her job was to find parents for little ones under the care of her department. When new adopters came to her, she wanted to do everything she could to guide them through the process successfully. Over the next 4-6 months, Sue would visit every two weeks to interview us, and build up a picture of us as a couple, and as prospective parents.

Sue called this 'The Form F'. Think Michael Aspel with that big red book (I was going to say Eamonn Andrews, but that makes me sound about 90 years old). The Form F is a written account of the whole of your life. This would 'form' the basis of a report which would go to an independent panel of people. They would then recommend whether or not we could adopt.

Sixteen years on, I read the document for the first time. It covers a myriad of different areas and is, at times, quite invasive. It gives details of our backgrounds: our upbringing, our parents, brothers and sisters, and our childhood memories. We both had to provide a family tree and information on the ethnicity of our wider families, providing photos wherever possible. This was all part of the matching process. A reoccurring theme of this process was that the child was front and centre of everything that was happening. Though we were looking to adopt to fulfil a need, Sue's role was to make sure the child had the best chance for a happy, positive life. The guidelines have changed a lot since 2004, but at that time the adoption team had to find the child a close physical match in terms of the parents' looks, skin colour and so on, so that the child was not made to feel awkward.

Our education and employment history was taken into account. I think this was really to get a feel for our thoughts on how we would support our child with their education, and what our work ethics were like. Reading back the section on myself, I was amused to see that Sue had written the following:

'Nick says, "I was someone who by and large thoroughly enjoyed school. I don't have many memories of my early days in junior school, other than my mum being called in as I had taken a strong dislike to my teacher. My mum says she thinks it was because the teacher had bright red hair and look scary.

I have many happy memories of my later years at St. Andrew's, particularly being given the leading role in the school play. This turned me from being fairly quiet and shy into a confident show-off and I think it was a big turning point for me personally. This meant that I could enter secondary school with much more confidence." '

Our interests and talents – I would like to have said that football was both an interest and a talent, but I'd be lying about the latter. On reading it back now, some sections of the report feel quite light, and not that relevant to why I should be allowed to adopt. But I can see that the overall objective was to build a full picture of me as a person, to allow a group of people, who had never met me, to decide on my future. I am still not quite sure how my love of karaoke could have swung things either way though.

The section on personality was very telling though and could still easily be used to describe me today:

'During the assessment process, Nick has presented as thoughtful, sensitive, intelligent, and articulate, methodical and cautious. He is honest and insightful and can recognise his own limitations and *vulnerabilities. Nick is a confident man with good self-esteem.*

Nick is aware that at times he uses humour to mask his emotions or to transfer anxious feelings, and this is something he has worked on during the assessment. Nick has been completely engaged with the assessment process and has learnt a lot about himself, such as the barriers he sometimes puts up to express his real feelings. I believe that his openness and flexibility will help Nick to be a really good father to an adopted child.

Nick can be initially reserved and quiet in new situations, preferring to spend time weighing things up but once he feels able to trust people, he is friendly and sociable and feels he is good at making and maintaining relationships.

It is important for Nick to be independent and self-reliant and he sometimes finds it difficult to ask others for help for fear of being seen as a nuisance. Nick is aware that he will need to be more open to support once a child has been placed with him and Lynn.'

We were also asked about our relationship, the result of which now reads like a script from 'Blind Date'. We work well as a couple as neither of us try to be the dominant partner. We share all the household tasks and are confident we could share parenthood in a similar fashion.

One area Sue did focus on a lot over that period was our support network. I do wonder how much consideration many couples give this when they can conceive naturally. It is a vital area for all parents. You can't stick your child in the kennels if you want a break from the 24/7 job of being a parent, so you need that support team to help you. For us, it was primarily grandparents, but family and friends also played a key part. We had to focus on the fact that things would get stressful. So, who could we rely on, for both practical help in terms of looking after the child and mentally, who did we have that we could talk to, vent out on or just go for a beer with? We were fortunate to have a great team around us already but being made to focus on it certainly helped us in the longer term.

During the assessment process, Sue met both sets of parents, as well as 'interviewing' Lynn's friend Lisa and my mate Gregg. We were not present at any of these meetings but were heartened by the fact that everyone said how well they had gone, and how they had told Sue just how amazing we would be as parents.

There were some very dull, but I suppose necessary, sections to the assessment, including the home safety check. I could not see how the fact that our front door was fitted with a multipoint lock would define what I was like as a father, but with hindsight, this was all about the safety of the child. You can see how the adoption team would have been crucified if they had allowed a child into a house where their safety could have been put at risk. Mostly it was common sense. We needed to child-proof door shutters to kitchen cupboards and plug socket covers, as well as install a couple of fire

56

extinguishers. It was a good thing that Sue had never seen the house when we still had holes in the kitchen floor. That would have been a real baby trap.

One of the hardest parts of the assessment was to give Sue honest feedback on our placement considerations. What we would or would not be able to consider in a child as their prospective parents. Some parts were straightforward enough; we only wanted to adopt a young child; 0-2 years old. We felt that an older child, more aware of their background and more likely to have suffered a troubled childhood, would be too difficult for us to manage. Plus, from a selfish point of view, after four years of trying for a baby, we did not want to miss out on those early years.

We also ruled ourselves out of taking on a child with significant medical needs. The list contained around 40 different scenarios. As we went down it, excluding one thing after another, it felt like we were seriously reducing our chances of adopting at all. However, Sue had been clear about this. Unless we were 100% certain that we could deal with a certain condition, illness or complexity, then we should say no.

There were some grey areas, which I would suggest to any new prospective adopters that they do their homework on, and those were the mental health aspects. Whilst these are often not yet diagnosable in a very young child, knowledge of the birth family can give an indication of potential issues. I had never heard of the autistic spectrum before, but there are so many different conditions within it. We had to accept that any child we may adopt could develop mental health issues over time.

Sue visited us religiously every two weeks from there on, through March, April and May, to build up the all-important dossier on us. We had a break from the meetings at the start of June as we were going to Devon with Jill, Malcolm and the kids. The timing couldn't have been better because, on 7th June 2004, we found out that Lynn was pregnant.

Chapter 11: Do You Believe in Miracles?

Well, this was unexpected, to say the least. While we had been in Devon, Lynn had told me that her period was late. With all the IVF treatment over the last couple of years, this wasn't unusual. However, this time, she felt different. Women's intuition. She bought a self-test kit and those two miraculous blue lines appeared. It was confirmed. After all those false hopes that we were going to have a baby and it had happened naturally. We had no idea how it had happened. Well, we did. I know all about the birds and the bees, but how had it happened now? It hadn't worked with the IUI, it hadn't worked with three of the four IVF attempts and even then, the 'successful' one was hardly that.

No, this was truly a miracle, up there with the feeding of the five thousand and turning water into wine. There were so many emotions all buzzing around at once. This had happened naturally, therefore the embryo had to be stronger than those artificially implanted during IVF. That meant it had to be a stayer, right? Lynn had also started to get cravings for orange Lucozade, so that was further than we'd gone before. Everything happens for a reason. Maybe our journey had happened so that we would truly appreciate our son or daughter when he or she appeared in a few months. All the excitement was countered by a feeling of guilt; what would we tell Sue? She'd think we had been wasting her time for the last four months, sending her on a wild goose chase while we knew all along that we were going to have a naturally conceived baby. How could we even tell her?

We made an appointment with our GP for the following Monday and he confirmed that Lynn was indeed around seven to eight weeks pregnant. He knew our fertility background and was genuinely happy for us after all the misery we had been through. But he also advised us to play it safe until we got to the twelve-week mark, just as he would have done for any normal pregnancy.

We got back home after that appointment and worked out our plan. We couldn't tell Sue just yet, as much as that felt like an unethical thing to do. We would carry on with the adoption process until week 12 was safely past, then we would confess.

Fortunately, there was a natural break in our sessions with Sue, as she was interviewing family and friends at that time. Therefore, we didn't have to tell her any lies. It was a strange few weeks. Euro 2004 was on the television, so I was able to take my mind off things for a few hours each day, watching Holland v Germany, Portugal v Russia and the always exciting Denmark v Sweden. England played a couple of matches during that time; a 3-0 win over Switzerland and a 4-2 battering of Croatia. A young chap called Wayne Rooney, just 18 at the time, was taking the competition by storm. I often wonder what happened to that lad.

The tournament was turning out to be as unexpected as our pregnancy, with Germany, Italy and Spain all knocked out in the group stages and France getting turned over by Greece. The only predictable thing was that England lost on penalties, only this time it was to Portugal rather than Germany.

Having kept the news to ourselves for a couple of weeks, we visited Lynn's parents on the weekend of the 19th June and couldn't contain ourselves. Our visits normally started with us arriving on a Friday evening, then sitting and chatting into the wee hours with several bottles of wine being consumed. The fact Lynn wasn't drinking gave the game away. That and her mother's intuition. As had happened 16 months previously, there were lots of tears of happiness and everyone agreed that as this had happened naturally, then it would surely be OK. We enjoyed our weekend by the sea and when we returned home on Sunday, which was also Fathers' Day, we went over to my parents in the evening to give them the good news too.

Everything was going smoothly until the following weekend. I'd been out with some of my workmates for a karaoke night on the Friday. Lynn sometimes came along too but she was feeling a bit under the weather, plus we didn't want loads of people asking why she wasn't having a drink, then putting two and two together. Saturday morning and something definitely wasn't right. Lynn had bad stomach cramps and that term I'd learnt to hate so much in the last two years came up again; 'spotting'. She had started bleeding on and off. Not so much that you knew things had gone badly wrong, but enough to bring that sick feeling back into the pit of your stomach constantly. This continued on and off over the weekend but seemed to ease up by Monday morning. We booked a doctor's appointment first thing, but they didn't have any windows until Wednesday morning, 30th June. The doctor, knowing our history, arranged for Lynn to have a scan first thing on Wednesday, then come into the surgery to discuss the results. Lisa had again covered for us, telling work that Lynn was off with a stomach bug.

With ironically apt timing, as soon as Lynn had the scan, the bleeding intensified. We made our way from the hospital to the surgery, knowing in our hearts that it was happening again, the cruellest of twists in our long journey so far. The doctor immediately sent us back to the hospital where, over the next few hours, our unborn baby lost its battle to survive.

The next few days were an emotional blur. The hospital had advised us that the baby would have to come out and Lynn needed to check each time she bled to ensure this happened. I use the term 'baby'. I know technically it was still just a foetus, but I still can't bring myself to use that word for our child. By that stage of pregnancy, the baby is as big as a strawberry, measuring about 1.2 inches long.

If losing a baby is not heart-breaking enough, having to search for its remains every day is a whole new level of pain. It was a task we both took on for a week, finding nothing. The same week, our friends Terry and Alison, now with baby Evie, were emigrating to New Zealand. Terry had been a big support to me over the last few years, always ready to go for a run or, more often than not, a beer when I needed to let off steam. A big chunk of our support network was disappearing when it was needed most, not that we wished them anything but the best for their exciting new adventure.

The following Wednesday, 7th July, we were back at the hospital for a follow-up scan. Just when we thought we had hit the lowest point we were pushed further into the abyss. Our baby was still in Lynn's womb. Dead but not moving anywhere. Therefore, the hospital would have to carry out a procedure known as dilation and curettage. I remember the doctors referring to it as D&C, and all I could think about was Dolce and Gabbana. It is a procedure to remove tissue from inside the uterus, if it has not cleared naturally, to prevent infection.

We were both still in a bit of a daze, but the gist of it was that we would come in the next morning for the operation which would only take 15-20 minutes. Lynn had to be sedated and would need some recovery time afterwards.

Thursday 8th July must go down as the most miserable day in my 47 years on this planet. We arrived at the hospital at 9.30 am and waited. And waited. And waited. We waited until 11 pm, when we were told by a very apologetic nurse that the operation wouldn't be performed that day. At least I had been able to have a sandwich for lunch; Lynn hadn't eaten all day. As we lived so close to the hospital, we opted to return home for the evening and try again tomorrow. The next day we were back in at 8.15 am and eventually got home at 7 pm. When the doctor told us that the operation had been a success, I could only think of how David Brent from 'The Office' would have handled the news much more tactfully.

We had the weekend to reflect on what had happened, and what we were going to do. We certainly couldn't tell Sue what had happened now. With all that had gone on, there was no way on earth that she would think we were in a fit state to carry on the adoption process. In fact, she would probably want to send us off for counselling and the whole adoption process would stall, and probably be stopped completely. No, we had to ride this out and we didn't have much time to get our game faces back on again as we were going to be attending a two day, assessed group adoption course in under a week.

Chapter 12: Back to School

Thursday 15th July. Just six days before, we had been mourning the loss of our unborn baby. Today I sat reading the course outline and the key areas for assessment. The main focus would be on our ability to manage anxiety, loss and grief. Oh, the irony of it all. I could give you a masterclass in that, Mr Assessor, but that would also end with me being kicked out of the class.

Mr Assessor was a social worker/facilitator from outside of the adoption team, though there were a couple of the Greenwich social workers there too. My initial impression of him was not good. He was dressed like the character Millie Tant from the old Viz comics, with a strange ethnic hat that looked like an upside-down tin of sweets that had been decorated by a clumsy child. With hindsight, neither Lynn nor I were in the right frame of mind to be in this group right now and Mr Assessor turned out to be a lovely guy. But there we were, and we were being assessed. We had to focus ourselves on passing and block out all the pain and sadness that had overwhelmed us in the last week.

There were four other couples with us on the course. We had not met any of them before and we made awkward small talk around the drinks table as we got ready to settle in for the day. It soon became clear this was going to be a tough day emotionally. I'd been on teambuilding type courses with work where you just say what you think the trainer wants to hear. This was very different, and I quickly saw that there was no hiding. Everyone was brutally open about what had brought them here today and hearing their journeys immediately built bonds of trust, unity and camaraderie between all of us. Everyone had been on the same path we were walking. Sometimes they had taken other routes, but they had all ended up here. It was both saddening and strengthening to know we were not alone, and these people were so compassionate when they heard our story. No one was afraid to share the most intimate things, no one was embarrassed if they got upset or tearful. Everyone was there for one another despite only knowing each other a few short hours, that first morning of the course. I remember at one point saying how unfair it was that we couldn't have children when these 'toe rags' were churning them out left, right and centre. I noticed a slight raising of eyebrows from a few people, including the assessor, and thought I'd put my foot in it. At one of the breaks, one of the other lads on the course, Paul, came up to me and laughingly congratulated me for going in 'studs up' and saying what he and his wife felt, but didn't want to come across as too harsh.

As I mentioned, the key objective of the course was to test our ability to manage anxiety, loss and grief, difference and contact. But not our feelings of these. No, this was where it was rammed home to us that the child was at the centre of everything. Yes, we were all sad and all grieving at not having children of our own. The social workers understood that, and admired and applauded our commitment to becoming adopters. But we now had to prove we could be the best parents those children could ever have, compartmentalise our own losses and help give them the best life possible.

The course was hugely beneficial and focussed us on what it meant to adopt a child. We had all been asked to bring an item of real importance to us. I took in my first ever watch that my nan had given to me when I was 5-6 years old. I have vivid memories of her teaching me to tell the time, and hiding away in the dark with it so I could look in amazement at its green luminous hands.

The assessor asked us all about our prized possessions. Then he took them from us and put them in a bin bag. He then chucked the bin bag out of the bloody window.

While we were all looking at him in stunned horror, he came back and asked, 'How does that make you feel?'

What he was trying to show us was that a child who has been taken from their birth family, for whatever reason, loses everything they ever had. All their attachments are gone. All they knew before is gone, and they are alone in the world. All they have are their memories. He went on to explain how it is so important not to change an adopted child's first name, even if you really don't like it yourself. The name they are given by their birth parents will often be the only thing they have left from them. It is not your right as an adoptive parent to take that away.

Incidentally, it turned out he didn't chuck the bag out of the window. He had switched bags with a sleight of hand that Paul Daniels would have been proud of.

So, the anxiety, loss and grief parts of the course were all about learning to support your child as they come to terms with why they were adopted. With very young children, this may not come to the fore for many years, but older children could arrive fully aware and very emotionally scarred by this 'rejection' by their birth families.

On the second day of the course, we did an exercise where our assessor had a big ball of red string. We all took on different roles: birth parents, extended family, social services, adoption agencies, adopters, magistrates and so on. He showed how these roles intertwined around two sisters at the centre of the scenario. By the end of the task, the 'children' were surrounded by a tangled web of around 200m of 'red tape'. It was a real eye-opener; a 'penny dropped' moment.

But that was not the end of the story. The children whose case we had been discussing were not made up, they were real, and in walked their adopted parents. There was a hush in the room as we all looked shocked. This was real, and these people had been through it all, but here they were beaming from ear to ear, so happy to meet us and share their story with us. They were fantastic to meet, and happy to share their contact details with us if we ever needed advice once we had also adopted.

The second day had focussed on difference and contact. Difference is the ability to empathise with your child and understand that they will at times struggle with the fact they were adopted. It was no longer acceptable to simply not tell them and hope no one else did. You had to be as open as possible with them and make them know they were loved. Anyway, what was 'different' nowadays? So many children now had birth parents who have separated and have new partners who are not biologically linked to them, but they are still mum or dad.

The contact element was the trickiest one for me; maintaining contact with the birth family. We had been apprehensive about this and had told Sue that face-to-face contact was something we would find hard. We were happy to do what was known as 'letterbox' contact, which was simply a letter once a year to tell the birth family how the child was doing. Again, it was made clear in the session that contact wasn't about our feelings, but how our son or daughter would feel if you cut out that route of communication because you didn't like it.

Ultimately it is a major consideration that an adopted child comes to you with all these connections and complexities, and that is before you have introduced any of your family and friends into the mix.

By Friday afternoon, we were a group of frazzled, emotionally drained but much better-informed couples. We popped over to a pub across the road to have a celebratory pint before going our separate ways. Although we had not been told, we all got the impression that we had passed the course and were ready for the real action to begin. It seemed a whole world away from just the week before, and whilst we still mourned, we had a renewed sense of purpose.

Chapter 13: He's Called Joshua

'Hi Nick,

We enjoyed having the chance to speak to other adopters last week as we can remember so well what it was like for us. Constantly grabbing at any information we could get and trying to understand as much as possible.

15 months down the line we now have 8 photo albums and reasonable life storybooks to recall the girls' earliest experiences. All the hard work though does pay off for all involved and gives you back your sanity. It hasn't been all smiles and laughter, but I still would never change a thing. We believe we have been made better parents than we would have been if we had been lucky to have had a natural family of our own.

There are a lot of good things adoption brings to you, the children are only a part of it.

Please keep in touch, and honestly, any help/advice we can give (even where to buy things, didn't get a chance to mention that last week) we are happy to oblige.

*0208****** - Home phone number... you may need to talk ...!*

Stefan'

I'd emailed Stefan after the course to thank him for his amazing help. Stefan was 'The Dad' in the red string exercise. I was so pleased to get the above reply and kept it in our Form F folder.

Being an adoptive parent puts you in a group. It's a lovely group. When you meet a fellow adopter, you just 'know'. It's unwritten, and there are miles of words that could be spoken, but you don't need them. We all know the struggles we went through to reach the summit.

On 21st July, we received official confirmation that we had passed our assessment and were being put forward to adopt. Sue didn't waste any time at all, bless her. On the 23rd July, we met our son for the first time.

OK, maybe that is being overly dramatic, but we did, in the form of a photo. I can still picture that moment as clearly as if I'd been in a delivery suite at a hospital. Sue had come over with 'news'. She had been working on a match in the background, concurrent to our progression through the process and course. We didn't know this and we were sitting in our back garden, with hearts in our mouths. You could tell that this was the bit Sue loved doing. She gave us a bit of background about his situation. He was 8 months old and had been taken into foster care the day he was born. It had all been preordained months before his birth. The birth family was 'erratic' and not able to cope.

Sue told us that she had some photos but was wary of showing them to us unless we realised the enormity of what this meant. She didn't want us to fall in love with a picture and just agree to everything if we were not sure. This was very much like one of those 'your house may be at risk if you fail to keep up repayments or any other loans secured against it' statements. We knew a baby was waiting for us and we knew there were pictures. It was a no brainer, show us the bloody photos.

Sue handed us the envelope and left us sitting in the garden while she retired to the kitchen to give us some space to think about what she had told us, and then if we were willing, to look at the photos. I'm pretty sure she was probably watching us from inside but at that moment everything around us stopped, all that mattered in the world was in that little white envelope I was holding. We looked at one another before I lifted the flap and eased out the two images. The first was an A4 sized print of a gorgeous, chubby little face, big brown eyes, the middle finger of one hand stuck in his mouth, mesmerised by the camera taking the picture. That was enough right there and then. This was our little boy.

The second picture was a glossy 6" x 4" photo of a smiling baby sat upright, dressed in a white jumper, with a little bear logo on it, and tiny jeans. He was looking at something just out of the photo. He looked so adorable. It took us a few minutes to compose ourselves before we could call Sue back out. She had deliberately not told us this little boy's name yet, in case we didn't want to go ahead. Giving us a name would make it too personal at that point, as if the photos weren't enough.

'Well, what do you think?' asked Sue. The tears of joy both of us were crying were enough of an answer for her. I think I eventually managed to squeak out a 'Yes!' and a nod of my head. Sue then revealed his name.

'He's called Joshua.'

Joshua. Joshua. Joshua. Yes, that was a fine name for our boy. We then learnt how he came to be named. His birth mum had been watching an episode of Friends while she was pregnant. Friends Season 4, Episode 13 'The One with Rachel's Crush' to be precise (Sue wasn't actually that specific, I found the details out later). Rachel met a guy called Joshua through her job and immediately fell for him. She went home to the flat that evening and stood in front of Phoebe, Joey and Ross, repeating his name over and over in different ways. That was enough to give Joshua his name. Given what we had been told at the adoption course the previous week, this was great news, in that it wasn't going to be a name we'd struggle to keep.

With Sue happy that we were absolutely on board with her choice, we made arrangements to meet up early the following week to get things underway. Sue would bring Joshua's own social worker with her, for us to be given a full briefing on his background, the conditions of adoption and the timescales involved.

That weekend, I turned thirty-one years old. We celebrated quietly what would be my last birthday as a non-parent. The following Monday, 27th July, Sue came over with Rick who had been working with

Joshua's birth family for some time. Rick was a striking character, dressed brightly, full of energy and excitement. It rubbed off on us straight away. He told us how Sue had come to him some weeks ago to tell him that we could be a potential match for Joshua. Rick had read our file and backed Sue's thoughts.

Though Sue had given us an overview of Joshua's situation, there was a massive amount we didn't know. Rick sat us down and went through everything. Joshua was the youngest of three children his birth mother had had. Of the two others the eldest, a boy, had already been adopted and his parents now lived in the USA. The younger child, a girl, was still with her birth parents, but it was a fluid situation.

Just as we'd found out during our chat with adopters back in September the previous year, the background story was very familiar. There were potential issues that may not be evident now with a young baby but could come to light further down the line. Again, this was another belt and braces warning, but we'd already seen him and fallen in love with the little fella. There was really nothing that Rick could say to us now that would deter us from pushing ahead with the adoption process. It was agreed that Sue and Rick would take the match to panel. The next morning, Sue sent over our completed Form F for review, more to pick up any glaring errors than for us to contradict what she'd said in it. We need not have worried on that front though, she had painted a very positive picture of us as potential parents, so good in places that I found it hard to believe I was reading about myself.

We got everything signed off, then were immediately off on a week's holiday in Gran Canaria with some friends; the last time we'd be going anywhere without a barrow full of children's necessities. It was a great week away. Joshua's photo came with us and took pride of place on the dressing table in our room. It was a week full of laughter, sunshine, beer, and karaoke. We spoke excitedly to anyone and everyone who would listen to us about our baby and how excited we were to meet him.

On our return a week later, we had a message from Sue. The adoption panel would be sitting in a week's time to decide if we would be approved as Joshua's new mum and dad. We knew it was going to be quick, but not that quick. It sent us into a bit of a panic, a happy one, but a panic nonetheless. Though most of the house was now decorated how we wanted it, we didn't have a shred of anything whatsoever for our baby. Cot, bedding, toys, clothes, spoons and bowls, bottles, pushchair, bathmat...nothing. It was all going to be a bit of a rush now. Yes, we'd been preparing for this for four years, but under normal circumstances, you would get a nine-month warning to get your arse into gear. I had also left the box room last on the list to be redecorated until we knew if we were having a boy or a girl, so that was going to need doing too.

Lynn's sister worked at Mothercare, which was handy, especially the staff discount, as we were going to need to spend a fair few quid to get everything we needed. Sue had told us not to go overboard on clothes and bedding as those things would come with him, but when it's your first baby you want to have everything how you want it. However, we had to be mindful of what we had learnt on the adoption course. This was not about us; it was about Joshua. He was about to be uprooted from everything he'd ever known so we had to do what we could to make that transition as easy as possible for him. That meant keeping all his existing clothes, his bedsheets and blankets, toys, teddy bears and his main feeding accessories.

12th August was upon us; D-Day. We had to travel to Greenwich for the panel meeting. I can't fully recall exactly how many people were on the panel, what they asked us or what our replies were. I just remember going into a council building feeling like I was heading into court to be sentenced. Sue had told us not to worry, we would be fine. She and Rick had crossed all the 'T's and dotted all of the 'I's, but after so many horrible failures in the past, we couldn't relax in the slightest. What if we said the wrong thing or one of the panel members took a dislike to us?

We went in at midday, for what seemed like an eternity, but when we came out it was only 12.20 pm. We were asked to leave the room while the panel members discussed the case. They told us to go and get a cup of tea from the canteen. Before we'd even been served Sue had come to find us, her face beaming. She only needed to say

'Congratulations' to us and I was off again, crying like a baby.

Chapter 14: Me, Myself and Irene

The initial excitement turned to confusion a little later. We were still not quite there yet, as we also had to be approved at a link hearing. However, we were assured that this was now just a formality and Sue wanted us to meet Joshua's foster mother, Irene, as soon as possible to start planning the transition process.

We arranged with Sue for her to bring Irene over to our house on 18th August. This was not just a 'meet and greet', it was also for Irene to feel comfortable that the little baby she'd been looking after like her own for 9 months was going to be taken care of.

If we'd gone overboard with tidying up when Sue first visited, Irene's impending visit sent us into overdrive. They were not due to arrive until 12.30 pm so we were up early with our cans of Pledge and Windolene. Everything was polished to within an inch of its life, nothing was left out of place. All the safety measures Sue had detailed during the assessment were in place, plug covers, cupboard door closures and the like. Even though it was the height of summer I had bought and installed a fireguard just to show how safety conscious we were. I guess the only trick we didn't use was to try baking bread before she arrived.

12.30 pm came and we welcomed Irene in. She was not like anyone I'd ever met before. She was a tiny Ghanaian lady with gold-rimmed spectacles, frizzy black hair, and an aura around her that exuded calmness, kindness, and authority. When she spoke, her voice danced over the words. I was immediately in awe of her and what she had been doing for our son. Irene was 60 years old and had fostered many children over the years. Joshua was to be her last before retirement, which made us even more nervous. We didn't want to let her down.

In the two hours Sue and Irene were with us, we soaked up as much as we could about Joshua and his routines, his habits, what he liked to eat and his fascination with opening cupboard doors. Brownie points for us that we could show Irene that our kitchen cupboards and drawers were more secure than Fort Knox. We gave Irene the grand tour of our house and showed her the box room which would be Joshua's bedroom. That was still looking a bit bare, but Irene didn't seem perturbed once I'd told her my grand plans for the tiny 6' x 6' space.

Because of timings and holidays, we were not going to be able to start the introduction process until the middle of September. It was a little frustrating, but it also gave us an extra week or two to make sure everything would be perfect. It was agreed that we would all meet in Greenwich on Monday 13th September. For our part, we were asked by Sue to create a little book for Joshua, containing pictures of the two of us. Irene would then start to introduce him to us gently so that when he finally met us in person, we would be a bit more familiar to him. We also needed to buy a small cuddly toy and keep it in our bed for a couple of weeks. This was so it would pick up our scents; it would then be given to Joshua and, as with the photos, it would give him some level of familiarity with us before we physically met him.

These were the little things we'd learnt about during our assessment, but finally being asked to do them felt big. Really big. This was real now.

A couple of hours after they left, I received a lovely email from Sue. In it, she said that Irene thought we were both lovely and she now felt much happier about letting Joshua go. It was then that it hit home just how hard it is to be a foster parent. To give your all to vulnerable children, knowing that they will be moving on elsewhere, wow. It was not something I could do. We were to learn over the coming weeks that Irene had that amazing ability to make a difference to the children she fostered and the strength to let them go to their forever homes. A truly remarkable lady.

Chapter 15: The Final Straight

The next three weeks were a blur of shopping, decorating, partying and golf.

During our assessment phase, I'd decided that I needed a hobby that would help keep me calm, so rather foolishly had picked golf. I guess it made sense in terms of being able to get out of the house for a few hours and enjoy the peace and quiet of the golf course, but what I hadn't factored in was that I was not very good at it. I started OK, but the more I practised, the worse I got. In those last few weeks, before we welcomed Joshua, I suddenly had the urge to practise as much as I could, in the misguided belief that I might suddenly see the light and become amazing at it. If anything, I plummeted to new depths. I genuinely believe that I remain the only person in golf history to have played a tee shot that landed behind where I'd started from. After that last hurrah, the golf clubs were consigned to the garage for the foreseeable future.

The partying wasn't exactly full-on Kanye West style, but we knew that once our little bundle of joy arrived we wouldn't be out and about for a while, so any chance we got to go out for dinner, have a few beers with the lads, generally get out and about enjoying life, that's what we did.

There was still a lot of work to do. I got stuck into decorating Joshua's room during weeknights and weekends. The good thing about a box room is that you can give it a makeover in next to no time. Wallpaper, paint and carpet all in place with relative ease. Far more painful was the shopping. Despite what we'd been told, and despite Irene also letting us know that there would be quite a bit of kit coming along with Joshua, Lynn decided to empty Mothercare of all its stock. She made a pretty big dent in Toys'R'Us too. I am surprised that both went bust if that was standard practice. We had a new cot which would convert into a bed later (thank God), bedding, cutlery, bottles, baby strollers and not one, but three pushchairs, one of which looked like a mountain bike on steroids. You name it, we had it. As for nappies, they were bloody everywhere I went. In the garage, the airing cupboard and under the beds. I thought she had bought enough to see this poor child into his teens. I later found out that what she'd purchased was actually only about three weeks' worth.

On 8th September, Lynn started her maternity leave. It was a very emotional day for her. She had been with her employer since 1985, joining straight from school. Many of her colleagues were also long-termers and had seen her grow up and had been there during her struggles to become a mum.

D-Day was fast approaching. On 9th September, the link hearing Sue had mentioned took place. We did not need to be present and as promised, it was a formality. The next morning, we received an official letter from the Adoption Agency Decision Maker to confirm the panel's decision. We had the all-clear to adopt Joshua.

Finally, the 13th came around. We drove to Greenwich to meet with Irene, Sue and the head of the adoption team, Florence, to work through the introduction plan which would run over seven days. On the eighth day, Joshua would be coming to live with us forever.

Chapter 16: The First Day of The Rest of Our Lives

Tuesday 14th September 2004. Just over five years (1,874 days to be exact) from our wedding day, we were finally going to meet our baby. We were not due to be at Irene's house until 10.30 am, but we left super early because we didn't want to risk being made late for any reason, plus we couldn't sleep anyway.

There are many things that I remember from this particular week in my life.

1) I came to know the journey to Greenwich like the back of my hand. For someone who struggled to drive anywhere further than a mile without the need for a map and directions, this was quite a feat and made me feel really grown up.

2) I became a fan of Chris Moyles, who was on the Radio One breakfast show at the time. He and his team became the soundtrack to our trips. Each day was filled with excitement but also fear, stress and worry. Listening to Chris chatting about anything and everything was great for helping take my mind off things and I'm still a fan to this day (he's now on Radio X if anyone else is interested, and can still chat away for 30 minutes plus without playing a record!)

3) I learnt that one sausage baguette for breakfast wasn't enough but two was too much. Each morning we would arrive way too early (better safe than sorry) and end up taking a walk about the local

vicinity to kill some time. We found a café that always seemed to be busy with lots of men in hi-viz jackets, drinking mugs of steaming tea and having full English breakfasts with side portions of chips. It became our local for that week and the sausage baguette became my staple diet. With ketchup, obviously. Anything else would be just wrong.

4) I hate going to Lakeside Retail Park with a passion. It has got way too many roundabouts, I could never remember where the car was parked, and the place is too busy and has too many shops that are not sports shops or off licences, which are the only places of interest to me in the world of shopping. We invariably ended up there each day on our way home from Greenwich, as Lynn was constantly remembering things we 'had' to buy for our new arrival.

On that first day, we arrived on the estate where Irene lived and had a job finding her block. From the outside, everything looked like flats, but Irene's house was a three-story townhouse-style build. After getting our bearings, we made our way through the front gate and up to the door. My heart felt like it was going to burst out of my chest, it was thumping so hard. I rang the bell at dead on 10.30 am and waited, listening to the slow and steady footsteps of Irene as she made her way down to the door. She was beaming as she opened the door to us and that made me feel a little less nervous. She fussed over us as we took our shoes off and welcomed us up into the living room.

It is a moment I will never forget. It's that moment I would have had as a new father in a delivery room at a hospital. The moment that fate and luck had denied me for the previous five years. The door was one of those that reminded me of school, with its glass panels reinforced with wire. It was half open and I could hear breathing and a shuffling sound on the other side of it, just out of sight. Slowly I edged into the doorway. On the floor in the corner of the room was my son, Joshua. Tears welled up in my eyes as I looked at him and then at Lynn, who was also starting to cry. Joshua on the other hand was seemingly oblivious to the fact that his forever mum and dad were here to see him. He was busy trying to pull a purple bow ribbon off the doors to the TV cabinet. Irene broke the spell by explaining to us that she'd had to tie the door shut to stop him from getting at the Sky box, which he was fascinated by.

We tried to compose ourselves. I even apologised to Irene for my tears. She laughed and told me not to be so daft and offered us both a cup of tea. It was her way of naturally removing herself for a couple of minutes to give us those precious first moments alone with our boy. We both sat down on the floor and watched with wonderment as Joshua, still indifferent to us, continued to tug at the ribbon, without success. I picked up one of his toys, a little electronic noise-making contraption, covered in brightly coloured buttons. I clicked a button with a cow on it and it mooed at me. Suddenly Joshua was taken away from his task and intrigued by his two visitors who were playing with his toys. He shuffled across the laminate floor towards us. When I say shuffle, that's exactly what he did. He didn't crawl as other 10-month-old children did. He sat, left leg tucked under his right, and scooted across the floor on his bum. We both started laughing, how cute was that? Irene came back in with a tray of teas. 'Is he doing his bum shuffle?' she asked, chuckling to herself. She'd kept that as a little surprise for us.

We only spent an hour with him that morning, but it was amazing. I took lots of pictures of him playing, and a couple of each of us with him. While he enjoyed playing with us, whenever we tried to pick him up for a hug or a picture, he'd quickly wriggle free. But it was OK, he didn't know us yet. He seemed to enjoy being with us and had even shown us the teddy bear we'd given him, the one we'd slept with. Irene also made a point of going through our little photo album with him while we were there, pointing us both out. It was a little overwhelming for the three of us but Irene, with all her experience in fostering, managed everything just right. She let us interact with Joshua and gently eased him back towards us when he naturally turned to who he thought was 'mum' from time to time.
We left Irene's on a high, so much so that I wasn't even disheartened by the prospect of a visit to Lakeside to have my credit card battered.

That night, as I downloaded those precious first photos and copied them on to disc, everything felt brilliant. It hadn't been the same as being in that delivery room, and I wasn't out smoking cigars or wetting the baby's head, but I was a dad now. I wondered what my little boy had thought of it all.

The next morning was very much a case of déjà vu. We drove to Greenwich, accompanied by Chris Moyles on the radio. We arrived way too early, so went to the same café again for sausage baguettes and tea. We even managed to get lost on the estate again before finding Irene's house, just in time to arrive bang on 10.30 am. Joshua seemed pleased to see us again, probably as he remembered these were the two strange people who played with him whilst crying at the same time. This time we managed not to cry and after an hour of playing, we left Irene and Joshua alone for a while so he could take a nap. We drove into Greenwich Shopping Centre and had a wander around until it was time to go back for lunch. Again, walking around that area felt odd, and I was constantly on the lookout for members of the birth family. This time it was even more real as Irene had shown us some pictures from Joshua's life storybook. The book began at day one and had several pictures of Joshua with both his birth mother and grandmother, taken in the hospital not long after his birth.

A life storybook is an important part of an adopted child's life and forms a bridge between their origins and their forever family. It is also a reminder to all of us that they have another family out there, even though their link to it is only biological, and that is the one piece of the jigsaw we were missing in all those years of trying for a baby. The other thing it did to me back then was make me feel a little bit sad for the moments we had already lost in the ten months Joshua had been alive for. His first Christmas was spent with Irene and her family. He went to Bognor Regis for his first holiday. We weren't there to witness his now infamous 'bum shuffle' for the first time. They were only little things, and we would still get our chance for firsts with him from now on, but it was another reminder of our journey to this point and how it was always going to be different. We'd not missed his first words or his first steps, his first day at nursery and school. There was still much to look forward to.

One thing I didn't look forward to was feeding time. On that second day, we returned in time to help give Joshua his lunch. Most of it ended up on the floor, the wall, the highchair; everywhere except his mouth. I didn't remember my niece and nephew being that messy, but he seemed to be enjoying himself. I thought of my newly decorated home and hoped he was simply putting on a show for us given it was our first attempt at feeding him. We left that afternoon, happy that we were beginning to build a bond with Joshua. We were only two days in, but it felt like we were making good progress. When we got back home that evening we popped over to my mum and dad's to show them the dozens of new photos we had of their first grandchild. They were even more excited when we said they would most likely be able to meet him at the weekend, now that the introduction process was underway and running well so far.

Day three started a little later, as we were going to see Joshua's evening routine. We still arrived crazily early, and for a change, I had a sausage baguette and tea for lunch instead of breakfast. We then went and fed Joshua his lunch, and I was pleased to see that the majority of it went into his mouth and not all over the kitchen.

After lunch, we took him out for a walk. This was another big step as it was the first time we had been alone with him. Yes, Irene had left us in the living room for a few minutes, but this was our first trip out as a proper family. We had brought one of our collection of pushchairs, and Irene seemed quite happy for us to use that. It was another first for me when I learnt just how much crap you have to take out with a baby, even just for a half an hour walk; spare nappies, bottles, wipes and an extra babygrow; the pushchair was filled to the brim like a comedy overloaded donkey. I felt that if I let go of the handles it would tip backwards with all the weight. Irene was lucky enough to live by a very picturesque lake which was ideal for taking Joshua around on our walk. We stopped and fed the ducks and pigeons and marvelled at this little boy's wonderment at the nature in front of him.

That afternoon we met with Dr Meerstradt, who worked with the Greenwich adoption team to review their children's medical history and advise prospective parents of possible health issues, both in the present and future. Whilst Joshua was normal in all physical senses, the pregnancy was not fully documented. His birth mother had gone missing for periods, had not attended check-ups and clinics when requested, and there was also a possibility of substance abuse, cigarettes, alcohol and possibly more. Dr Meerstradt explained to us that this was a potential minefield, particularly in terms of mental health issues that may only become apparent in the future, once a child had developed to a point where they were walking and talking. There could be any number of conditions such as ADHD, anything on the autistic spectrum such as autism, Asperger syndrome and other pervasive developmental disorders. Usually, these could not be diagnosed until a child was at least three years old.

It was all well and good telling us this now, and yes, Sue had also covered this area during the production of the Form F, but we had already met Joshua. He was bright, sweet-natured and as far as I was concerned, he was now our son. So, giving us this information seemed a bit irrelevant as it was not going to change our minds at all. Just give us the bloody baby.

After our meeting, we headed back to Irene's to take part in our first bath time. It was a bit surreal, with us crowding into the tiny bathroom with Irene, as she showed us the ropes then let us take over, but it was another thing ticked of the 'to do' list which needed completing before he could come home with us. I had only just overcome my fear of dropping the poor boy, now I had to try and not accidentally drown him. He didn't like sitting in those baby bath seats (of course, we had already bought one for home), so it was a case of keeping constant guard in case he tipped himself backwards.

We travelled home that Thursday night exhilarated. We were only three days in, but it felt like a lifetime already. We'd learnt a lot about our new son and we were already a bit too overconfident that this would be a doddle. We had another four days of induction to go, and this would be largely at our house. Joshua would get to meet all his family soon and everyone was excited about that. Sue told us to take it slowly and cautiously, and we wanted to, but we were also overwhelmingly excited to let everyone meet him. Lynn's parents were coming down for the weekend and we agreed as a sort of compromise that we would arrange for the family to meet him on Sunday, giving us Friday and Saturday to help him get used to his new house.

We got to have a lie-in on Friday, though sadly this meant I missed out on my daily sausage baguette. Sue brought Irene and Joshua over at midday and left them with us. It was a bit like taking a step back as Irene was once again in charge, but this was to help Joshua with the new surroundings. Whilst he had started to become used to us, he had never been out of his home without Irene. We gave him the grand tour, as much as you can do that with a 10-month-old. He was more interested in trying to get his right shoe and sock off, a habit that still puzzles me to this day; why only the right one? We introduced him to some new toys, as well as some familiar ones that we'd already started to shift across from Irene's. He seemed quite comfortable and even went exploring around the living room and kitchen on his own. I was pleased to see that my kitchen cupboard door locks held up to his attempts to break in.

On Saturday, Irene came over once again, this time with her son Sam, who for ten months had been Joshua's big brother. If you thought Danny De Vito and Arnold Schwarzenegger were an odd match in Twins, then Joshua and Sam were remarkable. Sam was around six foot four and built like a professional sportsman. Joshua looked like a tiny doll in Sam's arms, but from the way the two of them looked and laughed at one another, you could see they had a very strong bond. Just like Irene, Sam was so good with us, helping us with little hints and tips, and trying not to be the centre of Joshua's attention, even though it was clear that when Sam was about, no one else would get a look in as far as Joshua was concerned. Sam took his mum out for a look around the local shopping centre so we could spend some time with Joshua. We took him to our local park and that was where it felt real. We were home with our baby doing things that normal families did. We were both on a high that evening when we went for a meal with Lynn's parents.

Sunday was the big one. We were up and in Greenwich for 10 am to pick Joshua up, bringing him straight back home. It was going to be a busy day for him as he was on 'meet and greet' duty. It was another surreal time as one by one he met his family. First, it was Lynn's mum and dad, who were already at home. Joshua treated them with the same level of disinterest he had shown in us that first day, but that was largely because, as soon as he got into the house, he made a beeline for his toys. After we'd settled him in, Jill and Malcolm came over with Chloe and Alex. Now we had Joshua's attention. With two other children to play with, he really came into his own, giggling and clapping his little hands together as the kids messed about with him on the living room floor. Reluctantly we had to end playtime after forty minutes or so, as we were mindful of not overwhelming him, plus he was starting to get tired. He still had more visitors to receive later.

For me, the most emotional part of the day was seeing my parents and introducing them to their first grandchild. He was still half-asleep in his pushchair when they arrived and quietly moved into the living room to see him. It was a bit like an audience with the Pope, only Joshua didn't extend his hand for them to kiss. He waved his right sock at them as he managed to remove it for the fifth time that day. I did have to turn away and compose myself, as I knew if mum and dad saw me crying yet again, it would set them off too. Fortunately, my middle brother Paul had come with them and he is not one for standing on ceremony. He just wanted a beer and that gave me a bit of breathing space to sort myself out. Soon Joshua was up and about again, and my mum got her first hug. I even made him sit through his first-ever Spurs game that day, a 0-0 draw at home to Chelsea. My dad had made me a Spurs fan, so if I was going to suffer, so was my son.

Everything had gone perfectly that weekend, and Monday was also brilliant. We picked Joshua up at 9 am and didn't take him back to Irene until 4.30 pm. That night we celebrated our last night of freedom at a Chinese restaurant. Tomorrow our little bundle of joy was coming home for good, and it was going to be perfect.

Chapter 17: Coming Home

Tuesday 21st September 2004. Our final morning trip to Greenwich. My final sausage baguette and mug of splosh, as the lady behind the counter referred to it. It had been agreed we would collect Joshua at 10.45 am. Sue had advised us to make it a swift in and out, so as not to create a lot of upset for him. Irene and her lovely family had said their farewells to him the evening before, but after having him in their lives from his first day on Planet Earth, it was going to be an emotional time for them all. We felt it too. We owed Irene a huge debt of gratitude for looking after our son as her own for ten months and it was going to be upsetting seeing her in pain as we took him away from her. What compounded this was that it was Irene's last 'assignment' as a foster carer. Joshua was her final child, so it was going to really hit home for her when he was gone. Ever the professional, Irene shooed us off the premises (in a lovely way) before anyone could get too tearful. We could see she was upset, but she didn't want to burden us with that on what should be a happy day, and she didn't want Joshua to sense the emotion of the moment.

We left with our precious cargo and the remainder of his belongings and loaded the car up. Joshua quickly dozed off on the journey back and I remember checking my rear-view mirror every 2-3 seconds, not to look at the traffic behind me, but to look at this adorable, chubby chopped, squishable boy who was now coming to live with us.

When we got back home, we tried to keep things as normal as possible. There wasn't a big welcome party, instead, we drove to a nearby town to do a bit of shopping and took a walk around the park. When we got back, we fed him and gave him his first bath at home. Everything was running very smoothly. Then we tried to put him to bed. He was having none of it. We took him out of the cot and put him in the pushchair until he dozed off. We tried to take him upstairs again. No. He started crying. We brought him down again and back into the pushchair. Over the next three hours, we tried and failed several times to get him into the cot. Every time he fell asleep in the pushchair, one of us would try and remove him with the care and precision of Indiana Jones trying to replace an ancient crystal with a bag of sand, to try and avoid setting the inevitable booby traps off. Our booby trap was a screaming child and we set him off at least half a dozen times before we decided to cut our losses. At 11 pm, after a long day, we brought our bedding down to the living room and took a sofa each. Joshua seemed happy to sleep in his pushchair.

Chapter 18: It Wasn't Meant to be Like This!

After a fitful night of broken sleep, we were woken up at just after 6 am when Joshua stirred. Maybe we'd just had a bit of an off day when it had come to putting him to bed. After all, it was the first time we'd done it without Irene being around. We had probably been a bit too soft with him. We took him out to the shops in the morning and things seemed to be back to normal. Sue called to check on us and she agreed with our thoughts on why we'd had a tricky first night. However, that afternoon he cried non-stop for four hours. Nothing we could do would pacify him, and every time we tried to pick him up to comfort him, he would push back and struggle to get away from us. Eventually, he cried himself out and fell asleep around 6 pm, back in his pushchair. After the previous night with little sleep, we decided against trying to move him. Lynn went to bed at 8 pm and I was on Joshua patrol for the night. I got the bedding from the spare room and set up my bed on the sofa. I dozed off, drained, around 9 pm, but it was another night of restless sleep. I was up again at 5 am, feeling like I'd not slept a wink. When Lynn woke up, we agreed we'd have to take it in shifts to deal with Joshua. She would take him out so I could get a few hours' sleep. We called Sue and updated her. She didn't seem too worried by this turn of events but said she would come over that afternoon to check on us. She duly arrived at 1 pm and spent a couple of hours with us, reassuring us that this was normal. Joshua had not known anything other than life with Irene, so it was going to take him a little while to adjust.

Buoyed by our pep talk, we took Joshua over to my mum and dad's house for a few hours. It gave him somewhere new to explore, and Nanny had already bought a couple of new toys for him to play with. He seemed content but as the minutes until bedtime ticked by, we were becoming tenser. It was only the third night he had been with us, but we were both already feeling the effects of not sleeping properly over that time. Added to the emotional drain the whole situation had on us anyway, we were starting to feel down and deflated. This time we tried to take him upstairs at 7 pm but after one massive crying fit, which started before I'd even got him to the top of the stairs, it was back in the pushchair for the night. Not fancying a third night on the sofa, I moved the pushchair into the hallway at the bottom of the stairs, and we slept with the door open so that we could hear him if he woke. I say slept; I barely slept a wink. Every movement he made, I was alert and tense, waiting to hear the crying start up again. As it was, he slept through to 7 am the next morning, but another night of not sleeping properly was going to take its toll.

We tried to carry on with the shift routines during the day so we could take turns to get a bit of sleep, but it wasn't easy to doze off when you had the chance, no matter how tired you felt. I took Joshua to my work for something to do, and he really enjoyed bum shuffling around the offices and getting adoring looks from all the girls. All the parents I spoke to there told me not to worry about the crying and sleeping, it was something many of them had also gone through with their own children. The fact he was adopted didn't make a difference in their eyes.

That night we again tried to get Joshua up into his bedroom and into his cot, but once again he was hysterical by the time we had reached the landing. So, it was back into the pushchair and another restless night, waiting for the tears to start again.

By the weekend we were not in a good way. This was a massive mistake. We weren't cut out to be parents. Joshua clearly didn't like us or his surroundings, and he wouldn't let us pick him up or try to soothe him when he was upset. Lynn had taken it worse than I had in those first days. All her hopes and dreams of becoming a mum seemed to have been destroyed in a matter of days. She even wanted me to call Sue and ask her to take Joshua back to Irene.

I must have sounded pretty hysterical myself that Saturday morning as I called Sue. She wasn't officially working that weekend, but she had to use all her experience as a social worker to get me focussed. There was absolutely no way Joshua was going back to Irene. Firstly, he was not a toy or a dress that you could just send back for a refund. He was a human being who had been through a lot of trauma in his short life. Secondly, we had worked damned hard to get to this point, just to throw it all away at the first sign of trouble. Thirdly, Sue promised me that we were and would go on to be brilliant parents. She emailed me the following over to give us some sort of a plan to cope with the next few days:

'Let him see photographs of Irene and her family.

Sleeping is a very individual thing – all children are unique and what works for one child may not work for another. It will be trial and error as to what is going to work for Joshua.

You could try:
- *Having him in bed with you*
- *Having him in his cot in your room*
- *After a week, putting him in his cot and just letting him cry until he falls asleep*

You need to use Joshua's strong feelings to your advantage – by comforting him / holding him and keeping calm you will actually be encouraging him to trust you and helping him to feel safe.

This reaction may be partly to do with Joshua's temperament – some children withdraw, and other children come out fighting!

It is very important for you to understand that Joshua's distress is his way of expressing very painful emotions which he is unable to talk to you about. It is not a rejection of you, neither is any of this Joshua's fault or your fault – you are not letting anyone down.

Stages of grieving:
- *Shock*
- *Denial*
- *Anger*
- *Bargaining*
- *Sadness/Despair*
- *Resolution*

Most important of all, do not panic – this stage will not last, it just takes time.'

It hit me at that point that despite all the months of training and the intensive course, we'd totally lost sight of the main objective of adoption, and that was the child. With just a few nights of not sleeping properly, we were only thinking about us and feeling sorry for ourselves.

This poor child had been taken from one family and dropped into another, and we expected him to be all smiles and happiness about it. It was a culture shock to him. Irene's family were Ghanaian, Irene cooked Ghanaian food, most of the time she carried Joshua around on her back, tied to her with a sheet in a traditional African way. We were white, we cooked much less exotic food and we stuck him in a pushchair. All the faces, smells, experiences and comfort he knew and loved had been ripped away and replaced with almost the polar opposites. No wonder he was upset. Being unable to talk, his only way of expressing his pain was through crying and resisting our attempts to comfort him.

After another night in the pushchair, Sunday came, and Sue was on the phone to us first thing. She had a family she wanted us to meet. They had experienced a similar start to life as adoptive parents and had come through the other side. Happy to grasp on to any offer of help we could get, we arranged for Sue to bring them over that afternoon.

At 3 pm, Sue arrived with Maria and Bobby, who also had with them their two adopted children, Callum and Tom. Maria and Bobby probably don't remember much of that meeting, and we've not spoken to them since, but they really did help save us from ourselves that day. As we told them of our woes and how quickly we'd been brought down from the clouds into the depths of despair, they nodded knowingly. Their story mirrored ours, as did their feelings of that time. But they had fought through it and now had two lovely little boys who looked totally at ease and happy with life. Hearing how Maria and Bobby had won their battle gave us a bit more confidence to win our own. It was still hard, given that we were in amongst the muck and bullets right now, but we could see that it wasn't a hopeless task.

While Sue was with us, we showed her Joshua's reaction to being taken upstairs, if only to prove to her we were not mad or making it up. Her previous advice on sleeping had involved getting him upstairs. Sure enough, as soon as we got 2-3 steps up, he started crying, really distressed. No one had an answer for it, but we knew he couldn't stay sleeping in the pushchair forevermore. Sue suggested we set up the travel cot we'd inherited from Jill and Malcolm and put that in the living room. It wasn't ideal but it was a step in the right direction. He seemed OK downstairs and now he'd be in a cot sleeping properly and not propped up in the pushchair.

Chapter 19: The Cold War

My paternity leave was up now, so on Monday 27th September, I had to return to work, leaving Lynn to cope during the day. This also meant that our shift work approach was not going to work now. On a positive side, Joshua had slept from 7.30 pm the previous night until 6 am on Monday, without stirring. Knowing he was in a cot helped us sleep a little bit better too, though we were both suffering from tiredness. We still had no idea what it was about coming upstairs that upset him so much, but now we were even giving him his daily bath in the kitchen sink, rather than go through the screaming and crying fit that accompanied any trip up the stairs.

Going back to work gave me a bit of respite, but as we only lived a five-minute walk away from the office, I was going back for lunch most days to check up on things

Within the first two weeks, I noticed a change in Lynn's behaviour. She would literally be waiting at the door when I got home at around 6 pm each night, desperate to hand Joshua over so she could go for a walk or just go to bed. She was tearful, short-tempered and anxious. We'd only been a family for just under a month, but it was not turning out anything like we'd hoped it would. I would try to do what I could when I got home but I was not enjoying it either. This little child showed no interest in either of us, cried a lot, went mental if you tried to take

106

him up the stairs, and had to be washed in the sink! He didn't want us touching him, cuddling him or picking him up. All he wanted from us was food, he even struggled when we tried to change his nappy.

Social services had taken a back seat by this point. With hindsight, this was a bit of tough love. Sue's role in an official capacity was over and she had other prospective adopters to work with. She couldn't keep travelling across London to mollycoddle us. Rick was still involved while Joshua was still legally under the care of Greenwich, but parenting tips were not his thing and we didn't know him as well as we did Sue. We had to start to help ourselves. It was only later down the line that we realised Lynn was suffering from post-adoption depression. The following is cribbed from an Adoption UK factsheet on the topic:

'Post-adoption depression symptoms can typically appear around a month after placement, and research indicates that it shares characteristics with post-natal depression and minor to moderate depression, whilst also having some unique characteristics. In the past, its symptoms have been discounted as being similar to those of post-natal depression, because there is no hormonal aspect as a result of birth. However, a recent study has reported that there is no significant difference in the incidence of depression between adoptive and birth mothers.

Symptoms include either a consistently low mood or marked reduction in the feeling of pleasure accompanied by some of the following mental symptoms: anxiety, panic, inadequacy, being overwhelmed by responsibility, being slowed down, inability to get any enjoyment out of life, worthlessness, guilt, low self-esteem, loss of identity, loneliness.

Physical symptoms include aches and pains, stomach problems, back problems, sleep problems, tension headaches, lack of energy, fatigue, lack of concentration, forgetfulness, loss of or gain in appetite.

The adoption process is unique and very complex and creates a powerful mix of emotions, such as grief, loss, hope, expectation, anger, fear, joy, guilt – all of which run alongside the bureaucracy and legal framework related to adoption. Added to this can be feelings of frustration through having little control in what is a life-changing decision. A process which can last up to three years can take its toll both physically and mentally; and so, already, even before the challenges of placement, prospective adopters can feel worn down. Prospective adopters can be surprised to experience feelings of depression post-placement, just when their dream is finally being realised. Feelings of guilt and fear of being judged can prevent them from seeking help and support at this crucial time.'

With Lynn suffering, I went on to autopilot to try and keep things going. My sense of duty kicked in and I knew I had to deal with the situation even though I wasn't feeling great about things myself. I started to lean on the support network, asking my parents to take Joshua for a few hours here and there during the week when I was at work. Ideally, he should have been bonding with mum and dad, but seeing as he wasn't keen on that, Nanny and Grandad were happy to step in. The fact that they were not in a state of stress like we were also helped, babies can sense that sort of thing and react to it. Lynn's parents also started coming down to stay with us more often, again to help out and take the pressure off Lynn during the day. Lynn also took Joshua to stay with them in Margate for a few days here and there, which gave me a break.

We were making some progress. After several weeks of sleeping in the travel cot, we got Joshua into his bedroom. It was a real battle, done through a method known as controlled crying. We would put him into the cot and leave him for 5, 10, 15 minutes at a time. It was tough as the poor boy would really be sobbing, but you must leave it a set time before going to soothe him. Having him sleep that first night in his room was a big win for us. We suffered a few disrupted nights of sleep, but slowly he settled in and stopped being so afraid of the first floor of the house. Once he realised that there were new places to explore and new cupboards to open, that were not kept shut with Mothercare's finest drawer closers, he even began to enjoy being up there.

Things were beginning to settle down, but it was still not what I had envisaged life as a dad would be like. I was putting up with this boy who now lived with us. I didn't dislike him but certainly didn't have the feelings of love that I thought I would or should have. I was just getting by, day by day. It felt odd and I often questioned myself as to why this was. Surely I should be bonding with him by now?

In early November, just over seven weeks since she last saw him, Irene came to visit. It was a date that had been agreed back in September, but we were really worried about it given all the problems we had faced. It could be a disaster if Joshua saw Irene again and that sent us back to square one. We got in touch with Sue who was firm but reassuring with us. She made us think back to where we had been just 4-5 weeks previously and realise that we had made a lot of progress. She even convinced us that seeing Irene would be good for all of us and would reinforce our growing bond with Joshua.

Sue was right. Irene was brought over by Sam one Saturday morning for an hour. Joshua played with her and Sam but showed no signs of favouring her or wanting to go with her. It was another little win for us. Even if it didn't feel like it, he was getting used to living with us. We were a little fearful that night when bedtime came, but he went off without a problem. The next day, I took him to visit my nan, Mary. She was 93 years old and in a care home, suffering from dementia. It was a bittersweet meeting, sad but also very funny. Nan thought I was my dad and Joshua was me, but she had a lovely time talking to him. I have a couple of photos of the three of us together, Nan and Joshua looking totally confused whilst I sat beaming in the middle of them. I am so glad we made the trip that Sunday as two weeks later Nan passed away and my world began to unravel.

I'd always been close to my nan. My brothers and I used to take it in turns to spend the weekend with her when we were little, and we always loved it because we'd get spoilt rotten. As I got older and learnt to drive, I'd be Nan's chauffeur each week to take her shopping. She'd always try to pay me petrol money and despite my refusal, she'd tell me to shut up and stuff the money in my pocket. When she got too ill to live alone, I'd been the one who cleared her house out, because I knew it would be too hard for my dad to have to do it. Though she had been ill for several years, it still came as a shock when my dad called me to break the news of her passing. All the weeks I'd been functioning on autopilot, trying to keep our newly-formed family going, I'd been blocking out my underlying feelings. Finding out about Nan opened the floodgates. Referring back to the Adoption UK factsheet on Post Adoption Depression again:

*'Evidence clearly shows that fathers can also suffer
from post-adoption depression. In a study, fathers
described their depression in terms of anger resulting
from, for instance, failing to solve problems related
to the adoption, feeling let down by the
professionals, lack of proper information about the
child's history and lack of support. There are also
feelings of fatigue, lack of trust in their child and an
absence of mutual bonding.'*

I hadn't realised it, but I had also become depressed
and overwhelmed by everything. It came out looking
like an outpouring of grief for my nan, but it was
there in the mix.

It all came at what was supposed to be a time of
celebration with Joshua's first birthday coming up
four days later. We tried to make the best of it for
him, and it was a special weekend. We started off at
home after he'd slept through in his own cot and
took him on a mini-tour. After we'd given him our
presents and he'd sat and played with the wrapping
paper, we took him to my dad's work for an hour to
say hello to everyone, then back to see my mum.
From there we headed off to Margate so he could
see his other grandparents. He loved it as he got
spoilt rotten by everyone. We stayed the weekend in
Margate and on the Sunday Jill, Malcolm and the
kids joined us for lunch at a pub by the sea. It was a
nice couple of days away, but we had to travel back
home for the funeral the next morning.

I'm sure no one likes funerals, but I really cannot do
them. Even if I barely know the deceased, the sight

of those who loved them being so upset really affects me. That cold but sunny day in November when we laid Nan to rest was heart-breaking. We did have a tiny breakthrough that morning though, even if I didn't notice it at the time. We had to take Joshua with us as there was no one to look after him. He was next to me in his pushchair but was wriggling about when the vicar started the service. I thought I'd have to take him outside for a walk but instead, he wanted to get out. I scooped him up and sat him on my knee. I started to get tearful and subconsciously squeezed him for comfort. Rather than fight his way out of the hug, he let me carry on. It was almost as if he knew I needed support right at that time, and he would put aside his dislike of me for a short while to help me grieve. A truce if you like.

As we moved into December, I was slowly falling apart. Joshua had started waking up during the night and refusing to go back to sleep in the cot, so the pushchair had been redeployed. At least now we could bring it upstairs, so he was still in his room, but it started to become a habit, bringing back night after night of disturbed sleep.

I then got ill and had to take the best part of a week out of the office. Work was becoming another problem that was affecting my mental wellbeing. The owners had been working on five-year plans and for 2005-2010 had employed an interim director to come in and restructure the business, to take it to the next level. I had been on paternity leave when he had arrived and when I did get back into the office, I immediately felt this guy was not going to be good for me. He was all buzz words and impressed with letters after your name. That was not me. I had been working there for eight years and knew the business inside out, but I was not going to start pretending to be someone else to be part of the 'in-crowd'. This attitude was most probably exacerbated by my mental state in general, but I got it into my head that I was having none of his BS, and pretty much sidelined myself.

It was in December that we began the process of officially adopting Joshua. Sue was helping to guide us, but we were mainly dealing with another social worker who specialised in the process. The first thing she had tried to do was approach Joshua's birth mum to sign final consent forms to allow the legal process to begin. Unfortunately, she either wasn't up to speed on this particular case or hadn't read the forms properly herself, as she had asked for this consent on the day of Joshua's first birthday. It was hardly a surprise she did not get a positive response. This would delay things as the consent was required to apply for a freeing order, which in turn would trigger the adoption application. With Christmas on the horizon, it was likely nothing much would happen until the New Year.

It all felt a bit daunting. Yes, we were functioning as a family, but I still didn't feel I had a bond with my son. I was still just going through the motions each day, each week, and just getting by. I was feeling sorry for myself but wasn't telling anyone, certainly not anyone in the support network, because they all assumed that we were nicely settled now. After three months I should be, shouldn't I?

I kept it all bottled up until our work's Christmas party. I arrived in a foul mood, my work attitude problem fully on show. I proceeded to knock back half a dozen bottles of beer in the first half an hour I was there, skulking around, giving the interim director daggers whenever he came into sight. As the night wore on, I just wasn't in a party mood and sat on a sofa outside the main hall. One of the new girls from our office in the Midlands came over and introduced herself, Karen. I don't think she knew many people there herself and was trying to keep out of the way too. It was one of those chance moments. If she'd not seen me there sulking, we may never have spoken. But she did and suddenly I was unloading my story and all my fears to a stranger. Karen had two children aged 8 and 10. She listened to me, didn't judge, and even told me it was OK not to like your kids sometimes. It felt like a huge weight was lifted from my shoulders. What I was feeling wasn't strange or shameful. Karen told me to call her at the office whenever I needed to talk, and I will always appreciate that gesture. In terms of adoption in general, it also showed me that no matter what preparation you make beforehand, once you're in amongst the muck and bullets, no amount of planning can prepare you. You must take help from wherever it appears and be willing to adapt when needs be.

The next morning as I was trying to burn off those beers in the gym, this Robbie Williams' song came on my MP3 player (remember those?) and it resonated with me so much it brought me to tears:

'They're selling razor blades and mirrors in the street

I pray when I'm coming down, you'll be asleep

A young pretender and my crown's a broken seat

I come undone

I am scum

Love your son

You gotta love your son'

Chapter 20: Getting to Know You

Inspired by my party pep talk, and the prospect of a couple of weeks away from the office for Christmas, I promised myself I would enjoy the festive season and make the effort to really try and bond with Joshua.

Jill, Malcolm, and the kids were heading to Australia for Christmas to visit family, so Lynn's parents were coming to housesit for them. This was good as we would have them to help support us, plus Lynn's dad loved going to the pub.

Christmas day was split, with us visiting my mum and dad in the morning, then coming home to have Lynn's parents over. Once again, Joshua was royally spoilt. In between Christmas and New Year, he also had a couple of sleepovers with his respective grandparents. However, once January came around, I was again finding it difficult to deal with the situation. Talking about mental health issues was not a done thing in 2005. I hope that anyone in a similar situation to me now would find it a lot easier to get the help they need. I was slipping back, despite my best intentions. I would take the long way home from work at night, knowing that I'd be expected to take over the child-minding duties as soon as I got in. The long way home happened to have a pub on the route, and I soon became a regular for a pint or two after work. Nothing major, but it kept me out long enough that it would only be half an hour or so before bedtime once I eventually got back home.

While this was going on, the adoption application was progressing through the courts. It still didn't feel real, and by then I was just hoping that things would somehow sort themselves out, as I couldn't bring myself to tell Sue, or Greenwich, that I had these feelings. I guess I was a bit like a reluctant groom, standing at the altar, knowing the bride was coming, but not sure how to tell her I was having second thoughts. My sense of responsibility was stomping over most of my feelings anyway. I had made a commitment and I had to see it through now.

January flipped into February and a final adoption hearing date was set for the 21st. Lynn was excited, she had gone through the whole post-adoption depression cycle and had come out of the other side. She was bonding with Joshua now, as she was with him during the daytime, taking him to playgroups, forming new friendships with other mums and having coffee mornings.

On the other hand, I just saw him as the little sod who tried to wriggle free if I dared to pick him up or try and play with him.

We were coming up to deadline day when nature intervened in the most unpleasant but effective manner. On 17th February Joshua became very ill, he was constantly being sick, and he had very bad diarrhoea. The doctor said it was gastroenteritis. After a couple of days of this, Joshua was so worn out that he stopped fighting to get away when I picked him up. Taking this as a positive sign, I dived into helping with him, changing nappies, trying to feed him little bits here and there. Within 48 hours, I was suffering the same symptoms and was completely wiped out. The two of us spent the whole weekend laid out on the sofa and he snuggled into me as we watched TV. He couldn't escape me, and as much as it was no bundle of laughs for either of us, it proved to be a significant development in creating a bond between us.

The next day we travelled to the Inner London and City Family Proceedings Court in Wells Street, which is, ironically, just a stone's throw away from the London Women's Clinic in Harley Street, where we had been through those three failed IVF attempts two years earlier.

Neither Joshua nor I were feeling very perky. At least he had the benefit of wearing a nappy though. Our hearing was at 10.30 am and was attended by the three of us, both sets of grandparents, and Sue. The three magistrates in charge had no hesitation in granting us the adoption order. We were finally bona-fide parents.

I suppose I was happy, well happier than I had been a week before. I was starting to bond with the little man but there was still no thunderbolt moment, nothing where it all suddenly clicked in to place and I was a loving dad.

Over the next couple of months, we slowly built on that bonding which the gastroenteritis afforded us. It was more like a good pair of shoes, eventually after a bit of breaking them in, they become so comfortable that you forget you even have them on. 'Joshua' became 'Josh' or 'Chubbers'. We spent time in parks, or out by the seaside in Margate. We attended adoption support groups in Greenwich and were able to share some of our experiences with others, pleasantly surprised to see we were doing much better at this lark than we had thought. Irene came to visit to check on her boy and there was no negative reaction from him. We felt confident enough by then that there wouldn't be. Seven months had passed since he had joined our family. We now felt he was a part of it.

That thunderbolt moment did eventually happen, though it was more of a reasonably sized puff of smoke than a staccato lightning strike.

At the start of May 2005, I travelled with twenty or so of my mates from the football club for our annual end-of-season tour. This year we were heading to Albufeira in Portugal, for four nights. The first day was pretty frenetic with initiation drinks for newcomers, way too many beers and lots of over-the-top behaviour. For my own part, I arrived back at our block of apartments at 5 am, only to find that my key wouldn't open the door. I proceeded to kick the front door in (and believe me, they don't just cave in, like in the movies. I was kicking the damn thing for ten minutes before it gave way), only to find I was on the wrong floor and had just cost one of the other lads a new lock. Having sheepishly gone back down a floor and opened my own door with the key, I headed to bed. The next day I phoned home and my first question to Lynn was 'How's Chubbers?'

The next couple of nights when we hit the town, the single lads tried to chat up girls, but I was the one these ladies ended up talking to because I wasn't hitting on them. I just wanted to tell them about my little son who I was missing. Without realising it, I'd become a doting father. Finally.

Chapter 21: My Family

Life settled into a routine of normality from then on, with the occasional curveball. Not long after I'd returned from Portugal, I took a call from Sue. Josh's birth mother had had another baby. She had been born several weeks premature and was in intensive care. Mother and baby were not doing well, and Sue was sounding us out to see if we would consider taking another child on. We did discuss it a lot and felt that with everything we had been through, it would be a struggle. Neither were we sure of how such a premature birth would affect the baby. In the end, it wasn't a choice we had to make as it was decided that the mother and baby would be able to stay together this time.

That summer we took Josh on his first holiday. We travelled with my parents and my two brothers, Paul and Tim, to the Isle of Wight. We stayed in a gorgeous thatched cottage in Godshill. It was so stunning that we soon realised it was one of the most photographed buildings on the island. Most mornings we opened the curtains to find groups of tourists outside, taking photos. A couple of times, I took Josh out wearing a pair of sunglasses and let him enjoy the attention of the tourists laughing and asking for photos of him too.

Further confirmation of my bond with Josh came in October of that year, Halloween in fact. In the early hours of the morning, I was awoken by a screeching noise coming from downstairs. I got up and was at the top of the staircase trying to work out what was going on. I realised that someone was trying to prise the front door open; the screeching sound was the UPVC frame, straining against the pull of a crowbar. I'd never been in a situation like that before, and I hope I never have to experience it again. Fight or flight mode. I went full fight. I was overwhelmed with rage at the thought of someone trying to come into my house where my son was sleeping. I had to protect him. It was such a fierce feeling in my chest. As the door finally gave way and opened, I screamed a mouthful of obscenities and launched myself at not one but three men in the doorway. I must have been a frightening sight as they instantly turned and fled down the street. I hammered after them and almost caught one before the adrenaline burst subsided. My thoughts immediately turned to Josh and I rushed back to make sure he was OK. He had slept through the whole lot and was none the wiser.

The police came round, and it was only when I was sitting giving them a statement that I realised I'd broken a toe. The incident made up our minds that we needed to move house. It took a few months, but by the end of June 2006, we'd sold up and had an offer accepted on a new property on the other side of town. It needed a lot of work doing so my parents kindly invited the three of us to stay with them. We ended up being there for almost five months, but it was a great time for Josh, and he coped with the move admirably. After a lot of hard work, we moved into our new home on Bonfire night 2006. A fresh start for our little family.

A year later, in November 2007, we contacted the Greenwich adoption team again. We were ready to go once more, despite all our ups and downs the first time around. Our second experience of adoption was so much easier. As we had already gone through the approval procedures and were 'old hands', the timescales were much reduced. By May 2008 we were meeting our new daughter, Lily, for the first time. We were bracing ourselves for another rough ride, but Lily fitted seamlessly into the family. It was only when she got a bit older that the fireworks started, but that is a story for another day.

Chapter 22: Epilogue – Things They Didn't Teach you at Adoption School

While I was doing my prep work for this book, I spent a lot of time stressing over how much anonymity I should give my family. Initially, I changed their names, but that seemed daft as I only ever expected people who knew me would want to read my story, and they all know our names. I wondered whether I should say we had adopted from Greenwich or keep things vague. With only 4,000 or so adoptions per year, stating where Josh was born would give the birth family a big clue to who I was writing about, if they happened to read this book. But then what are the chances of that?

There are many things that I cannot write here about his birth story, it would be unfair of me to do so. It is his story and not for me to tell.

Over the years, I have been asked hundreds of questions about adoption. Most people were like I was back in 2003 when our doctor at the Homerton hospital suggested it as an option for us. I had so little idea of how it worked, or more importantly, why it worked. If you have stuck with the story to this point, then I am assuming you might be interested as to what some of those questions were, and what I think the answers are.

Is it hard to adopt?

Yes and no. If you really want to do it, then you'll go through hell and high water to reach your goal. At the time, it didn't feel it was that intrusive or heavy going, but by the stage we were undertaking the assessment, we'd been beaten up so much by our quest to start a family that we'd almost become immune to the sticks and stones life kept hurling at us.

How much does it cost to adopt?

It doesn't cost anything money-wise, in fact, you can get grants and access to funding if you would struggle financially. The cost is more emotional. You have to open yourself up to strangers, and leave yourself totally vulnerable, as part of the process of understanding why you are adopting and who it is for.

Did you consider surrogacy or adopting abroad?

It never crossed our minds. To me, both of those ideas sound very American. And costly. Surrogacy would have been odd as we would have only been able to use my sperm, not Lynn's eggs. I don't think that would have been fair on her to have a child that was half of me and none of her. Besides, he would have been crap at football.

As for adopting abroad, again that just feels like a 'Brangelina/Madonna' thing to do. A noble thing, but also (to me anyway) a 'we have tonnes of cash so are showing you all how philanthropic we are' thing.

Are the kids able to speak to their birth families?

No, not directly. The 'rules' of adoption are that a child cannot be given details of their birth family until they are 18. We maintained 'letterbox' contact with both Josh and Lily's birth mothers for several years, but never received anything back. Social services arranged for us to meet Josh's birth mum shortly after we adopted him. We thought it was the right thing to do but every time a date was set, she went AWOL. The level of contact varies depending on the agreements put in place by the social workers in the beginning, and these will depend on many factors surrounding whether it is healthy to maintain a degree of contact or not.

The real game-changer around the subject of contact is social media. When we adopted Josh it barely existed, but now a quick search on Facebook can dig up birth parents and their families within a few minutes. In many cases, birth families do not know where in the world their birth children have been adopted, or what their new identities are (i.e. surnames) but adoptees and their families know the details of the birth family, so in theory, they could seek them out even though it is not advised. It is an area that the adoption teams and parents of today must battle with in as sensitive a way as they can. When we adopted, all forms of contact were administered by the adoption team, now it would be almost impossible for anyone to stop a curious adopted teenager seeking out and contacting a birth parent online, and that may not end well.

Do you feel like Social Services are watching you all the time?

Not forever. There were times during the assessment process where it felt as if they were digging into everything and anything, but I totally understand why that is necessary. They were deciding the future of a child and they had to make sure they did everything they could to ensure that the child would have the best chance of a happy life. The most intrusive part was after we had first taken Josh home but had not officially adopted him. We had to report to Greenwich if we took him to the doctor and we couldn't take him out of the country; it was like he was on remand from prison. On one occasion Lynn rushed him to hospital, and Social Services were on the phone to us before we'd had a chance to call them. We felt like criminals.

However, once the adoption order is signed, Social Services move on to the next, leaving you to it. They were still there in the background, and in fact still are there for us now, if we need them.

It's so brilliant that you adopted, you must be proud to be making a difference in the world.

People will often tell me how wonderful it is that we adopted, an act of selflessness to make a child's life better. OK, it is in one way, but ultimately there were selfish reasons at play too. We had a hole in our family, and we couldn't fill it ourselves. We were not Brad and Angelina, using our wealth to make a difference. We couldn't conceive a child, so we adopted one. At no point on the journey have I ever remotely felt like I was doing this for a noble cause. I grew to understand that adoption was about the child, not the adoptive parents, but the urge to be a parent was still a key motivator all the way through.

Does an adopted child feel like your 'real' child?

Yes, I've been asked that. Some people don't realise how insensitive certain words can be. 'Real' is a particularly nasty term. Real implies that you are an imposter, just filling in until the 'real' birth family can come back in and take over again. It's not like that at all. OK, the 'real' parents spent maybe ten minutes conceiving, and then the 'real' mother spent nine months carrying the child, but that is where it ended. Being a parent isn't just about having a baby, it is about raising and nurturing a child; teaching them right from wrong, feeding them, clothing them, comforting them when they are sad, going to parents' evenings, playing football in the park, letting them put makeup all over your face (yes, I quite enjoy that one), holding their hands, kissing their hurt better, teaching them to ride a bike, taking them to their first football match and watching them at their school play. If you are reading this as a parent, be it your biological child, stepchild or adopted child, you will know that the list is endless and that your job as a parent never stops.

I have never had a biological child so I cannot say with 100% certainty that there is no difference in the feeling, but many conversations with my friends over the years convince me that once you are a parent, you are a parent. There are no differences.

What do you think about their birth families?

This is a really tricky one. For me there is a level of resentment to both children's birth families for acting how they did, making the choices they made, not looking after themselves by abusing their bodies with cigarettes, alcohol and worse. All these factors have harmed my children and made their lives more complicated than they would otherwise have been. I can't judge them though, as I have not walked in their shoes. I had a fantastic childhood. I never went without and was always cared for by my parents and family.

I always remember my dad saying to me that babies are like a blank canvas and you can teach, influence and guide them to become the kind of people they should be, but adoption opened my eyes to the fact that so much goes on in that nine months in the womb. Not just physically, but mentally. In chapter 16, I described our meeting with the adoption team doctor who advised us that Joshua could have several mental health issues. At the time we dismissed it, as we just wanted to take him into our family. If we had our time again, we would have looked a lot more at that aspect, so that we would have been better prepared, and understood what we were possibly letting ourselves in for. Not so much with Josh, although he was diagnosed with Asperger's around the age of four, and we had two or three difficult years with him. Lily, however, is a different proposition altogether. Her mental health issues mean she had to leave mainstream school, and her behaviours and habits put the family under constant stress. There are days that you think 'what if', but ultimately there are many parents with biological children suffering much worse than we are, and it could have turned out exactly the same for us if we had a biological child.

Appendix

Adoption Statistics for year ending March 2019 – CoramBAAF –

https://corambaaf.org.uk/fostering-adoption/looked-after-children-adoption-fostering-statistics/statistics-england

Adoptions from Care

3,570 looked-after children were adopted during the year ending 31st March 2019

Awaiting Adoption

4,330 children had an adoption decision but were not yet placed at 31st March 2019

2,800 children had a placement order but were not yet placed at 31st March 2019

Waiting Times

433- the average number of days between a child entering care and moving in with its adoptive family during the year 2018-19

173- the average number of days between an LA receiving court authority to place a child and the LA deciding on a match to an adoptive family during the year 2018-19

Adopter Characteristics

During year ending 31st March 2019:

88% (3,140) of children were adopted by couples and 12% (430) by single adopters

14% (490) of children were adopted by same-sex couples (either in a civil partnership, married or neither)

Printed in Poland
by Amazon Fulfillment
Poland Sp. z o.o., Wrocław

62202858R00080